SNEAKING OFF WITH GOD

TORN CURTAIN PUBLISHING
Wellington, New Zealand
www.torncurtainpublishing.com

© Copyright 2023 Simon Dodge. All rights reserved.

ISBN Softcover 978-0-473-69926-0
ISBN EPub 978-0-473-69927-7

No portion of this book may be reproduced, stored in a retrieval system or transmitted in any form or by any means—electronic, mechanical, photocopy, recording or otherwise—except for brief quotations in printed reviews or promotion, without prior written permission from the author.

Unless otherwise noted, all scripture is taken from New International Version®, NIV®. Copyright © 1973, 1978, 1984, 2011 by Biblica, Inc.™ Used by permission of Zondervan. All rights reserved worldwide.

Scripture quotations marked NASB are taken from the New American Standard Bible®, Copyright © 1960, 1971, 1977, 1995, 2020 by The Lockman Foundation. Used by permission. All rights reserved. lockman.org

Scripture quotations marked NLT are taken from the Holy Bible, New Living Translation, copyright © 1996, 2004, 2015 by Tyndale House Foundation. Used by permission of Tyndale House Publishers, Inc., Carol Stream, Illinois 60188. All rights reserved.

The Essential 100 Challenge™ (The E100) is a registered trademark of Scripture Union Inc., and is used with permission.

Cover photography by Simon Dodge. Used with permission.

Cataloguing in Publishing Data
Title: Sneaking Off With God: A guide to finding intimacy with God through the Bible
Author: Simon Dodge
Subjects: Christian living, prayer, bible study, discipleship, spiritual growth, bible study methods, pastoral resources, devotional resources, inspirational.

A copy of this title is held at the National Library of New Zealand.

SNEAKING OFF WITH GOD

A guide to finding
intimacy with God
through the Bible

Simon Dodge

CONTENTS

Introduction		1
Chapter 1	What I Want More than Anything in the World	3
	SOAP: God's Love Surrounds Me	5
Chapter 2	Intimacy with God	7
	SOAP: The Gracious Hand of God is Upon Me	9
Chapter 3	Humility and Hunger	11
	SOAP: Humility Takes Courage	14
Chapter 4	Conformed to His Image	16
	SOAP: Failure is Not the End	18
Chapter 5	Meeting with God in the Bible	20
	SOAP: Lord, What Have You Got for Me in This?	22
Chapter 6	What is SOAP?	25
	SOAP: The Quiet Place	27
Chapter 7	S: Scripture	29
	SOAP: Breathe and Be Breathed Upon	31

Chapter 8	O: Observations	33
	SOAP: The Ultimate in Designer Clothing	38
Chapter 9	A: Application	40
	SOAP: When the Dam Breaks	45
Chapter 10	P: Prayer	47
	SOAP: Grace is the Antidote to Disgrace	54
Chapter 11	Taking SOAP Further	57
	SOAP: Self-Talk: The Power of Life and Death	59
Chapter 12	Complementing SOAP	61
	SOAP: The Colour of Heaven	63
Chapter 13	SOAP is for Sharing	65
	SOAP: A Gentle and Humble Heart	67
Chapter 14	Other ways to SOAP	69
	SOAP: Pause	71
Chapter 15	Hot Bread and Honey Dew	73
	SOAP: Fruit of a Life Well Spent	78
Epilogue	Starting a New Habit	80
Author's Note		81
Recommended Resources		82
Appendix 1: Understanding the Structure of the Bible		83
Appendix 2: How to Read the Bible		85
Appendix 3: The Essential One Hundred Challenge		90

INTRODUCTION

This book is about intimacy with God, and how to find it. In particular, it's about meeting with God in the Bible using a technique called SOAP, which is an acronym for Scripture, Observations, Application, and Prayer. Since I started using SOAP, my own relationship with God has grown deeper and richer than I could ever have imagined. I don't put that all down to SOAP, yet this discipline regularly and reliably brings me—with open ears and an open heart—before the God I have come to love, and it can do the same for you.

One of my favourite characters in the Bible is Enoch. His story is found in Genesis 5 where, in the middle of an otherwise matter-of-fact genealogy list, he alone is singled out because of his relationship with God. Not much is said about Enoch in those few verses, but one thing is mentioned twice:

He walked with God.

When I die, I would love for people to say the same thing about me: "He walked with God." Yet something more is implied by these four words. Not only did Enoch walk with God, but God walked with Enoch.

What a beautiful and remarkable picture of the relationship God wants with us—not a distant or far-off relationship, but a continually deepening friendship cultivated by regularly walking and talking with Him.

For all who seek to know God (or to know Him more closely), the invitation to walk with Him remains open. All may come, for God does not discriminate. Yet of one thing we can be sure—no one who enjoys such a walk with God can remain unchanged. This is the blessing of intimacy with God. To walk with Him is to know Him, and to know Him is to be transformed with "ever-increasing glory" into the likeness of the One who has chosen to walk with us (2 Corinthians 3:18).

Throughout this book you will find a selection of SOAPs written over a number of years. Many of them are personal favourites which I include as examples of SOAP, though what they really illustrate is what my own SOAPs look like. Your

SOAPs will likely look different, since they will reflect you, the way you express yourself, and where you are at in your journey with God. So rather than making comparisons, just make your SOAPs your own, since, in essence, SOAP is simply a means to an end—that is, that you might draw close to God, and have Him draw close to you.

My prayer is that *Sneaking Off With God* will inspire you to pursue intimacy with God and give you the practical tools to achieve it. God bless you in your pursuit of Him!

ONE: WHAT I WANT MORE THAN ANYTHING IN THE WORLD

One of the fascinating things about us human beings is that we are all so different. What one person might love, another can detest.

Take running, for example. Some people regard running as something to be avoided at all costs, except perhaps in the most dire emergency, such as running away from a bear or dashing for cover in a hail storm. But me, I love running. I do it for fun and have enjoyed it for as long as I can remember. In primary school, I narrowly beat my friend Gary to win the school cross country race. The captain of our world-champion rugby team, the All Blacks, shook my hand at the finish line. It's still one of my greatest claims to fame. I think running must be in my genes.

It's not just the physical exercise I enjoy, but the places running takes me. I love to get out into nature. I love to explore and to photograph the beauty of the natural world. I also relish the opportunity to fossick and collect things. Stones, driftwood, shells, even the odd rustic fence post . . . all sorts of treasures find their way home with me when I'm out running.

But though I enjoy those artworks of nature, my favourite treasures have generally come from a little further 'upstairs', because something wonderful happens when I go for a run—my brain goes for one too. And what freedom! Unlike my body, which is fixed in time and space, my brain is free to roam wherever it likes. Like a dog at the beach—remove the leash and it's off!

Recently, I had just such a run. I was up on the hills rounding a corner by a great rocky outcrop when something caught my attention. I turned to look. *What was it?* No, not the sweeping vista of tussocky hills, nor the windswept beauty of the harbour below. It was a swallow. I watched in awe, marvelling at its aerobatic prowess— so graceful, so agile—and off went my mind, unleashed. *That swallow is like the Holy Spirit,* I thought to myself. *He catches my attention when I'm not expecting it. Brings a thought into my mind. Gives me a nudge. Prompts me, somehow. Sometimes He's subtle. Is that God?* I ask myself. But I know it's Him.

So, I respond. And the more often I respond, the more attuned I become to His presence. *I'm getting the hang of this*, I like to think to myself. *This is how the Holy Spirit moves! Like a swallow. Graceful, agile, subtle . . .*

But not always subtle, I have discovered. In fact, sometimes He moves less like a swallow and more like a shovel in full swing.

One day I was reading in Matthew's gospel and got to the part where Jesus says, "Ask, and it will be given you. Seek and you will find. Knock, and the door will be opened to you" (Matthew 7:7). I had read that passage countless times before, but on this occasion, *Wump!* It hit me like a smack in the chest with a coal shovel. Rarely had God spoken to me so clearly and so powerfully. I knew without a shadow of doubt that God was making me an offer: "Ask, and it will be given to you." I was stunned.

God once gave King Solomon the same opportunity. Solomon asked for wisdom, but I wasn't about to copy him. This was my moment. *What do I want more than anything else in the world?* I needed to think.

So, I went for a run. Near to my house flows a beautiful spring-fed stream. Its waters run crystal clear, and as I run past I often think of those well-known words of David from Psalm 23:2: "He leads me beside quiet waters." That day, running along the banks of the stream, I carefully weighed up my thoughts and desires until finally my mind was clear and I knew how I would respond to God's offer. Right then and there, I knelt down beside the trail and gave Him my answer: "Lord, what I want, more than anything else in the world, is intimacy with You."

SOAP #1 GOD'S LOVE SURROUNDS ME

Reading: Psalms 28-32

Scripture

Many are the woes of the wicked, but the Lord's unfailing love surrounds the man who trusts in him.

Psalm 32:10

Observations

The Lord's unfailing love surrounds me. His loving kindness envelops me like a bubble. The very air I breathe is infused with His love. God's unfailing love is my squad of bodyguards—in front of me, behind me, and beside me.

I can't accidentally stumble my way out of God's love. I can't lose it in the dark, and the dark cannot take it from me.

God's love for me is complete. I can't, either by effort or by prayer, gain any more of God's love, but I can gain a fuller appreciation of it. And I can be changed by it. I can become more aware that at every moment of every day, God's love is surrounding me.

Application

- *When I'm at work, God's love surrounds me.*
- *When I'm pottering around at home, God's love surrounds me.*
- *When I'm talking with friends, God's love surrounds me.*
- *When I'm having a disagreement with someone, God's love surrounds me.*
- *When I'm frustrated, God's love surrounds me.*
- *When I'm lying on the ground taking a picture of a toadstool, God's love surrounds me.*
- *When I'm asleep, God's love surrounds me.*

Prayer

Lord, knowing that Your love surrounds me somehow changes things. It changes the way I think. It changes the way I feel. It changes my expectations. Things are going to work out well. If Your love surrounds me, then wherever I am, Your love is there too. That has to be good, not just for me, but also for the people I am with. Your love accompanies me into every situation. Thank You for the wonderful privilege of knowing Your love. I want to know it more! I want to completely absorb it so that Your love flavours my whole being. My heart is open.

TWO: INTIMACY WITH GOD

I love the word intimacy. It sounds like "into me see." And that is exactly what it is! Intimacy is the closeness we share with another person when each of us is completely open and transparent with the other. *Into me see.* The guards are down. There's no pretending or hiding or covering up. Whether it be good or bad, embarrassing, or even painful, everything is visible and laid bare.

True intimacy requires courage. Being open and honest with someone can make you vulnerable. You could be hurt, embarrassed, or even rejected. But the closeness and connection achieved by such openness is unmatched; it breeds confidence, freedom, trust, joy. *"Into me see"* deepens a relationship like nothing else. Incredibly, God not only wants us to experience this kind of relationship with other people; He wants us to experience it with *Him*.

But is it really possible to enjoy intimacy with God Himself? I could answer this question for you from my own experience—*"Yes! It is possible!"*—but ultimately, you'll need to answer it for yourself.

Do you want to know God only from a distance, or are you ready to earnestly seek Him?

James urges us to seek closeness with God, and gives us a promise too, when he says,

> *Come near to God, and he will come near to you.*
> James 4:8

Jesus gives us this same assurance. In Revelation 3, He addresses the church at Laodicea saying,

> *"Here I am! I stand at the door and knock. If anyone hears my voice and opens the door, I will come in and eat with him, and he with me" (v. 20).*

These words were not written to those who were far from God but to believers who were struggling, and they paint a remarkable picture of the friendship that Jesus seeks with us. He doesn't insist that we come to His majestic dwelling place. Instead, having made us holy by His death on the cross, He has no qualms at all about coming to *our* place. He is pursuing us! He wants to spend time with us, and to break bread with us right where we are.

In his epistles, Paul describes Christ's pursuit of us as a bridegroom pursuing his bride (Ephesians 5). "All things were created by him and for him" (Colossians 1:16), and that includes us! Jesus made us for Himself, that we might be His bride. There is no relationship more intimate than the one between husband and wife. But even the healthiest marriage is merely a shadow—a picture, or *type*—of the relationship that we are being welcomed into with Jesus. The more we study the Bible, the clearer it becomes: We were created for intimacy with Jesus.

The same is true regarding our relationship with God our Father. The closeness of a good and loving father with their beloved son or daughter is available to all who open their hearts to Him.

How great is the love the Father has lavished on us, that we should be called children of God! And that is what we are!
1 John 3:1

Likewise, the Holy Spirit desires intimacy with us. In fact, He is the One that enables it, since He is not only close to us—He lives within us (John 14). The extravagance and wonder of all this is difficult to fully comprehend, and yet the message is clear: God wants intimacy with us, and there is no catch.

So how should we respond? What can we do on our part to move towards this relationship that God is seeking with us? I believe there are two things that open the way to true intimacy with God—humility and hunger.

SOAP #2: THE GRACIOUS HAND OF GOD IS UPON ME

Reading: Nehemiah 1-2

Scripture

"And may I have a letter to Asaph, keeper of the king's forest, so he will give me timber to make beams for the gates of the citadel by the temple and for the city wall and for the residence I will occupy?" And because the gracious hand of my God was upon me, the king granted my requests.
Nehemiah 2:8

Observations

Nehemiah recognised that the favour shown to him by the king was not because of the king's inherent generosity. Neither was it due to his own virtue, luck, or good fortune. It was, in his words, because the "gracious hand of my God was upon me." Nehemiah had prayed and prepared, knowing that ultimately, it was God who was going to make things happen.

Application

Knowing that God is the source of every good thing changes everything. If I need physical provision, I should ask God. If I need something to happen, I should pray. If things don't initially seem to be going my way, I shouldn't despair, because the gracious hand of my God is upon me, and things will ultimately work out well.

Grace means 'undeserved favour'. I do not receive grace because of my own virtue but because of Jesus who took my sin that I might enjoy God's favour.

Every good and perfect gift is from above, coming down from the Father of the heavenly lights, who does not change like shifting shadows.

James 1:17

If you, then, though you are evil, know how to give good gifts to your children, how much more will your Father in heaven give good gifts to those who ask him!

Matthew 7:11

And we know that in all things God works for the good of those who love him, who have been called according to his purpose.

Romans 8:28

What, then, shall we say in response to this? If God is for us, who can be against us? He who did not spare his own Son, but gave him up for us all—how will he not also, along with him, graciously give us all things?

Romans 8:31-32

Prayer

Thank You, God, for Your grace—for Your gracious hand resting upon me. I trust You for Your favour upon my marriage. I trust You for Your favour upon my children. I trust You for Your favour upon my business. I look to You for provision. My hope shall be in You as the source of everything that is good in my life.

THREE — HUMILITY AND HUNGER

You will not find intimacy with God without two things: humility and hunger. Humility is the phone call God always answers, and it is the key to intimacy with Him. God *always* responds to humility. Nothing warms His heart more than a person seeking Him with an open humble heart. Just search the words 'humble' or 'humility' in your Bible and you will quickly discover that from beginning to end,

> *God opposes the proud, but gives grace to the humble.*
> *James 4:6*

Jesus embodied this attitude, berating and lamenting the arrogance and pride of the religious leaders of His day whilst stooping to raise the hopeless from their despair.

When it comes to humility, there is one ultimate role model—Jesus Himself,

> *. . . who, being in very nature God, did not consider equality with God something to be used to his own advantage; rather, he made himself nothing by taking the very nature of a servant, being made in human likeness.*
> *And being found in appearance as a man, he humbled himself by becoming obedient to death—even death one a cross!*
> *Philippians 2:6-9*

What Jesus did makes one thing absolutely clear: In the Kingdom, humility is not just for the lowly, but for everyone. Shortly before His crucifixion, in a beautiful illustration of humility, Jesus washed His disciples' feet and then encouraged them to serve one another just as He had served them. "Whoever wants to become great among you," Jesus told them, ". . . must be your servant" (Matthew 20:26). About Himself, Jesus said,

> *I am gentle and humble in heart.*
> *Matthew 11:29*

He also said, "Anyone who has seen me has seen the Father" (John 14:9), making clear that our human expression of humility ultimately has its origin in the very nature and character of God. God is humble, and given that we are made in His image, it's no surprise that as we grow more like Him, one of the qualities that shines ever more brightly in us is humility.

That's a good thing, because when it comes to relationships, humility is the great enabler. Much of what Paul in Galatians 5:22 calls the fruit of the Spirit—love, joy, peace, patience, kindness, goodness, faithfulness, gentleness and self-control—is enabled and supported by humility. Love, for example, can never be complete without humility. Neither can patience or gentleness or compassion thrive in anything but a humble heart. It's humility that helps us let go of the need to always have our own way, enabling us to honour others above ourselves and to serve and bless people regardless of their situation in life, or ours. Rather than making us timid, humility brings confidence and poise by freeing us from the fear of what other people think. Our humility can also give courage to others by letting them see that we are safe to open up to, freeing them to be themselves. In all these ways, humility serves to strengthen relationships and create the conditions for intimacy.

The same is true of our relationship with God. To be humble before Him is to recognise that He is the Creator, and we are His creatures. Ultimately, we are in His hands, and only with humility can we be truly open and honest with Him about the state of our heart. Many things can keep us from closeness with Him—pride and pretence, missteps and misdemeanours, arrogance and self-sufficiency. Even the barriers we put up to protect ourselves from being hurt can prevent us from enjoying closeness with God, and it takes great courage to acknowledge these things. But courage and humility make great partners; together they help us to acknowledge our brokenness, and so permit God to gently heal us as hurts are unwrapped and wounds carefully uncovered before the great Physician. Healing is such a wonderful benefit of intimacy with God, and it begins with humility.

A humble heart is also a teachable heart, which is of great value in God's eyes. Being open to receive and learn from God enables Him to transform the way we think and respond to the events of our life. Instead of reacting to them, we learn to walk through them with God, 'unlearning' our old ways of thinking and instead seeing things as He sees them. Much of what we receive from God will come through our open teachable heart. It's hard to receive if our arms are full, but if we humbly lay before Him everything we hold—the good, the bad and the ugly—then our arms are freed up to receive fresh blessing and revelation from Him. Receiving from God is one of the great blessings of intimacy with Him, and it starts with humility.

Yet we need more than just humility. We need to be hungry. We need to *want* closeness with God, and to believe that it's attainable. In Hebrews 11:6, we read,

> *. . . without faith it is impossible to please God, because anyone who comes to him must believe that he exists and that he rewards those who earnestly seek him.*

Seeking God *earnestly* means to come to Him sincerely, fervently, persistently.

Intimacy with God is for the hungry.

It's for people who desire to be close with God more than anything else in the world.

In the Psalms, David expresses for us so well what it looks like to long for God above all else. He cries out,

> *O God, you are my God . . . earnestly I seek you; my soul thirsts for you, my body longs for you, in a dry and weary land where there is no water.*
>
> Psalm 63:1

Time and again, we encounter David's hunger and witness the depths of his longing.

Listen to his heart's cry in Psalm 42:

> *As the deer pants for streams of water, so my soul pants for you, O God. My soul thirsts for God, for the living God. When can I go and meet with God?*
>
> vv. 1-2

This is the kind of cry that moves the heart of God, because nothing delights God more than to feed the hungry!

So, are you hungry? Come, then! Press into God. Open your heart to Him. Seek closeness with your Creator, and you will find not only that God welcomes you with open arms, but that as your intimacy with Him grows, something else rather wonderful is happening too—you are becoming like the One you have drawn close to.

SOAP #3 HUMILITY TAKES COURAGE

Reading: 2 Kings 5

Scripture

Now Naaman was commander of the army of the king of Aram. He was a great man in the sight of his master and highly regarded, because through him the Lord had given victory to Aram. He was a valiant soldier, but he had leprosy.

2 Kings 5:1

Observations

I like Naaman. The writer describes him as 'valiant'. Other words for *valiant* are: brave, fearless, courageous, plucky, intrepid, heroic, stout-hearted, lion-hearted, manly, bold, daring, audacious, gallant, confident, spirited, unflinching, determined, stalwart, staunch, indomitable, resolute, steadfast, firm, unyielding, unbending, unfaltering, unswerving, unwavering, dogged . . .

I like those words! What a wonderful way to be described. Yet Naaman was not always valiant. When Elisha sent a messenger to instruct him to wash seven times in the Jordan, he was dismayed and angry. After a brief time, however, he came around, because it was in his character to be humble. Humility takes courage, and for Naaman, part of being valiant was being prepared to humble himself. Humility enabled him to overcome both the fear of appearing foolish and the fear of what others might think.

On two occasions in this story, God makes allowances for Naaman's imperfections. He allows him time to get over his disappointment before he finally obeys, and He agrees to overlook one aspect of Naaman's job requirement, which was to accompany his master to the temple of his pagan god. God sees Naaman's character, and He loves him.

Application

Humility is for the valiant! Rather than a sign of weakness, it is a mark of courage. Humility neutralises my fear of what other people might think, freeing me to do the right thing, and opening doors that the proud will never go through.

Lord, I see, too, that humility attracts Your favour. Even my missteps are not fatal when my desire is to please You. You know my heart.

But Lord, how does humility work in practice? How do I action it?

When fear wells up in your heart about what other people might think, turn your thoughts to Me. That fear is the perfect opportunity to worship Me by treasuring My opinion above all others.

Prayer

Lord God, I do want to treasure Your opinion above all others. May every inclination of my heart be towards You. As with Naaman, help me to be valiant and humble.

FOUR CONFORMED TO HIS IMAGE

In the Bible we learn two essential facts about God: God is love, and God is holy. To meet God is to come face to face with both attributes, and when that happens, it is simply impossible to stay the same.

Consider God's love. How can I experience God's perfect, unconditional love and not feel totally loved and accepted? What claim can shame or unworthiness have on me when God Himself loves me? *None!* In the face of God's love, they completely lose their foothold.

Paul expressed this reality when he prayed that the Ephesian believers would:

> *... know this love that surpasses knowledge—that [they] may be filled to the measure of all the fullness of God.*
> *Ephesians 3:19*

The implication is clear: to be rooted and established in God's love leaves simply no room in our lives for anything that is not of Him.

And what of God's holiness? How can I stand or even kneel in the presence of a holy God and keep clinging to sin? It is impossible. All my hidden sins and faults begin to fluoresce brightly under the UV light of God's holiness. "Please Lord, take them away! I don't want them anymore," I cry out. It's the only appropriate response—other than to run away. Yet His love compels me to stay.

Job experienced this. By all accounts, he was a good man. Yet when confronted with God face to face, he became acutely aware of his own unholiness, and he wanted rid of it!

> *My ears had heard of you but now my eyes have seen you. Therefore I despise myself and repent in dust and ashes.*
> *Job 42:5-6*

It seems that when the light of God's presence shines into all our dusty corners, there comes a sudden desire to clean the house! Fortunately, God is very happy to help. This is the beauty of intimacy with God. To meet with God is to be transformed, and the closer the intimacy, the greater the transformation. But for this to become our reality, something else is required: vulnerability. Intimacy requires openness on the part of both people in the relationship; it requires us to let our guards down with one another. Openness like this can be scary. It can make us feel vulnerable and defenceless, afraid that we might get hurt. Can we really trust God with the deep things in our hearts? And could this vulnerability really be mutual in a relationship with God? Could God actually become vulnerable before us mere mortals? Surely He has nothing to fear by opening His heart to me? *Does He?*

Enter Jesus.

At the climax of His time here on earth, He stood before His accusers, silent. Condemned to death, He was stripped, and flogged to within inches of His life. He was mocked and tormented. A crown of thorns was placed on His head. Then He was taken to the hill called Golgotha and crucified. Arms wide open, He hung on the cross, naked, while soldiers gambled for His clothes. People came to look. Some of them shouted,

> *Come down off the cross, if you're the Son of God!*
>
> *Matthew 27:40*

But He didn't come down. He stayed there until the moment He could say, "It is finished!" Then He died.

With that scene in our minds, let us ask the question one more time: *Could God ever open Himself up to such an extent that He would make Himself vulnerable to us?* Yes. It happened at the cross. In laying His life down for you and me, Jesus opened His heart wide with the ultimate invitation to "into me see." And what was revealed? What did we see there?

Love.

If you ever have any doubts that God wants intimacy with you, just remind yourself of Jesus at the cross. Yes, God has most definitely opened His heart wide to you—and He calls you to come. Listen to His invitation:

> *Come, all you who are thirsty, come to the waters; and you who have no money, come, buy and eat! Come, buy wine and milk without money and without cost. Why spend money on what is not bread, and your labour on what does not satisfy? Listen, listen to me, and eat what is good, and your soul will delight in the richest of fare.*
>
> *Isaiah 55:1-2*

So, are you hungry? Come. Come and let us look together at how we can find intimacy with God through the Bible.

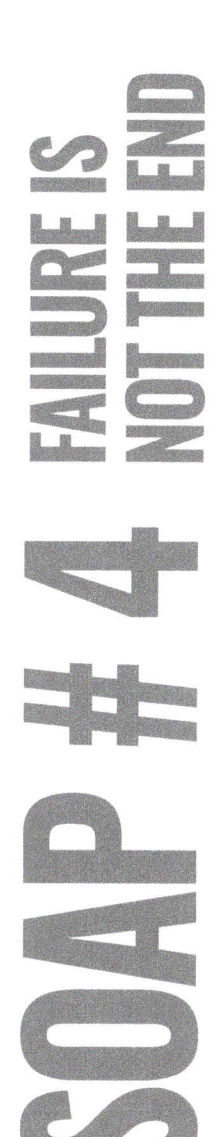

Reading: Mark 14-16

Scripture

"Don't be alarmed," he said. "You are looking for Jesus the Nazarene, who was crucified. He has risen! He is not here. See the place where they laid him. But go, tell his disciples and Peter, 'He is going ahead of you into Galilee. There you will see him, just as he told you.'"

Mark 16:6-7

SOAP #4 FAILURE IS NOT THE END

Observations

"But go, tell his disciples *and Peter* . . ." Peter, who just three days earlier had done what in his mind was unthinkable, disowning Jesus, not once but three times, just as Jesus had predicted. How must Peter have felt during those three days, after having so emphatically insisted, "Even if I have to die with you, I will never disown you" (Mark 14:31)? Did he have the courage to even let himself be seen by Jesus as He hung on the cross? I suspect not. He had stepped up to the plate and failed, dismally.

But Jesus knew. He knew Peter's despair and the bitter anguish of his soul, and on the cross Jesus bore in His body not only the failings of Peter, but the failings of us all. Soon, Peter's despair would be replaced by hope, and the angel was there to announce it: "Go, tell his disciples *and Peter* . . ." It's okay, Peter. You failed, and Jesus specifically wants you to know that He still loves you.

The redemption that Peter subsequently found in Jesus through that failure was, in many ways, the making of the man who would go on to lead the early church. Eventually he would even go on to make good on his promise, "Even if I have to die with you, I will never disown you."

Application

In the Kingdom of God, failure is not the end. In many ways, it's a beginning. It's an opportunity for me to stand before God with empty hands and acknowledge once again that He is my everything. It's an opportunity for my heart to be softened and prepared so that hope can spring up afresh and arrogance make way for graciousness.

Prayer

Lord, You know all too well that I have yet to reach a place of humility like the one Peter found himself in. But I pray that You would continue to perfect holiness in me as I journey with You, and if I meet failure along the way, please help me to grow from the experience, and to pass through it as one who has tasted more deeply the riches of Your grace.

FIVE MEETING WITH GOD IN THE BIBLE

I was a teenager when I first had the urge to pick up a Bible. It was a Good News Bible with a maroon hard cover. In my mind's eye, I can still see the simple line-drawings which illustrated the stories. (I like pictures; they stick in my head.)

Next, I bought a brown leather pocket New Testament so I could read whilst out and about. I even began memorising the odd verse. Then I discovered an old black King James Bible on the bookshelf at home that included a reference system alongside each verse. This changed how I read the Bible, opening a world of topics and verses I hadn't known existed. It was like following trails of jellybeans, each leading to a gingerbread house. I ate the jellybeans *and* the house! Finally, I decided to splash out and buy my own NIV Thompson Chain Reference Bible. This became my go-to Bible for the next twenty-five years.

I am still hungry for the Bible. But what exactly do I hunger for? And what did I hunger for as a fourteen-year-old? It wasn't information—though I did want to learn more about God.

What I really longed for was to connect with God; I wanted to feel close to Him. Interestingly, the more I ate, the more my appetite increased. I felt like Jeremiah the prophet who said,

"When your words came, I ate them; they were my joy and my heart's delight, for I bear your name, O Lord God Almighty."
Jeremiah 15:16

Like the writer of Psalm 119 who declared:

"How sweet are your words to my taste, sweeter than honey to my mouth! I gain understanding from your precepts; therefore I hate every wrong path. Your word is a lamp to my feet and a light for my path . . . Your statutes are wonderful; therefore I obey them. The unfolding of your words gives light; it gives understanding to the simple. I open my mouth and pant, longing for your commands."
Psalm 119:103-105, 129-131

Job was hungry too. He said that he treasured the words of God's mouth more than his daily bread (Job 23:12).

Jeremiah, the psalmist, and Job all had something in common—a voracious appetite for hearing from God. They wanted to know Him and to hear His voice. They were the spiritual equivalent of teenagers sneaking back to the kitchen an hour after dinner to hoover up some more bread. They were hungry! God's Word was like food for them, and without it, they were famished!

Why, then, if reading the Bible is like eating food, do we sometimes find it so hard to do? We're like Westerners trying to eat noodles with chopsticks for the first time. Is there a knack to it that we just don't know? The Bible is a very thick book. Perhaps we're just daunted by the size of it and don't know where to start—or how to start. Is it really possible for the average person to read and digest the contents of this book?

You would be forgiven for thinking that reading the Bible is like trying to eat grass. If you or I were to go out into a field of lush green grass and begin to graze, we both know what the result would be. Bellyache! Humans cannot digest grass! But take a look at cows. In New Zealand where I live, cattle are grass-fed. A typical Angus bull weighs in at 850 kilograms—now that's a lot of beef—and they get that big simply by eating grass. How can that be? What is their secret?

Actually, there is no secret. Cows ruminate. After an initial chew to get things started, they swallow the grass down into the first chamber of their four-chamber stomach for some initial digestion, then bring it back up to their mouth so they can chew it over some more. Nothing is lost. Gradually, the grass makes its way through their gut until the cow has extracted every last bit of goodness from it.

That's exactly what we want to do when we read the Bible. We want to ruminate and chew it over to extract the maximum benefit out of it. That may seem like a challenge, but my hope is to give you the knife, fork, spoon, or chopsticks you need to tuck in and enjoy the Bible for all it's worth. As you learn to feed yourself from this wonderful book, ruminating on it like a prize Angus bull, you'll soon be extracting more goodness from your Bible than you ever thought possible!

SOAP #5: LORD, WHAT HAVE YOU GOT FOR ME IN THIS?

Reading: Psalm 118

Scripture

In my anguish I cried to the Lord, and he answered by setting me free. The Lord is with me; I will not be afraid. What can man do to me? The Lord is with me; he is my helper. I will look in triumph on my enemies.

Psalm 118:5-7

Observations

This psalm celebrates the fact that with God, we are victorious. *I am victorious!* But there is no victory without a fight. You don't emerge victorious from a picnic. You don't triumph over a life of ease. You triumph over enemies and difficulties and trials. I note that the psalmist had experienced his fair share of these:

- *"In my anguish I cried to the Lord, and he answered by setting me free"* (v. 5).
- *"The Lord is with me; he is my helper. I will look in triumph on my enemies"* (v. 7).
- *"It is better to take refuge in the Lord than to trust in man"* (v. 8).
- *"All the nations surrounded me, but in the name of the Lord I cut them off"* (v. 10).
- *"I was pushed back and about to fall, but the Lord helped me"* (v. 13).
- *"The Lord has chastened me severely, but he has not given me over to death"* (v. 18).

Enemies, anguish, being surrounded, being pushed back and about to fall, being overwhelmed and overstretched, being tired and weary, being under the pump and under the weather, and even experiencing the discipline of God—these environments are the soil in which I grow. To know God as my strength, I need first to be weak. To savour the sweetness of triumph, I need to be fighting a battle. Salvation comes to those who need to be saved. Refuge is for those needing shelter.

- *Without a battle, there will be no victory.*
- *Without grief, there is no need of comfort.*
- *Without neediness, there is no need for provision.*
- *Without weakness, there is no need for strength.*
- *Without adversity, there is no need for refuge.*
- *Without despair, there is no need for hope.*
- *Without loneliness, there is no need for friendship.*
- *Without weariness, there is no need for rest.*
- *Without turmoil, there is no need for peace.*
- *Without uncertainty, there is no need for faith.*
- *Without danger, there is no need for protection.*
- *Without the need to be saved, there is no salvation.*

- *Without darkness, there is no need for a light.*
- *Without difficulty, there is no need for help.*
- *Without an unsure way forward, there is no need for a guide.*

Application

Lord, everything that happens and every situation I face is an opportunity to discover for myself another aspect of Your character, and to put my roots deeper into You. Knowing something in theory is merely a shadow compared with knowing from experience. Knowing that You are the Comforter, for example, is a shadow compared with experiencing Your comfort for myself.

So, rather than being dismayed or perplexed or frustrated at life's events, I can ask You, "What can I learn about You in this, God? What treasure is hidden in this situation? How can I know You better in this?"

Questions like this are the natural response of a renewed mind, where the reflex action is to trust You, God, and look for Your purpose. They take the focus off the situation and onto You. They're also the opposite of the victim mentality which complains and frets and despairs, asking questions like, "Why is this happening to me? When is it going to stop? How can I make it go away?" Rather, every challenging situation becomes an opportunity for intimacy with You—to know You more and to know 'more of You more'.

Prayer

This is such a fresh way of looking at life! It changes my whole expectation of what my life should contain and the value I place on my various experiences. My natural inclination is to want life to be easy and enjoyable and for everything to go well. But to know 'more of You more', it would be better if my life contained a good variety of difficulties and challenges. I imagine, the more difficult, the more valuable. Not that I'm asking for difficulties! But God, I do want to know You more, and I do trust You. So, as difficulties come my way, help me to see them as they are—opportunities to know and experience You more deeply.

SIX: WHAT IS SOAP?

Have you ever played the old party game "Pass the Parcel?" Inside that parcel, there's treasure, but it's wrapped in layers and layers of paper. As the music plays, each person passes the parcel to the person on their left, and round and round the circle it goes. If you're lucky, the music stops while you have the parcel and you get to unwrap one layer. But then the music restarts and the parcel is gone—who knows if it will stop with you again.

We can feel the same way about reading the Bible. There's treasure in there, for sure, but sometimes it just seems so hard to unwrap. You feel like saying, "Stop the music, I want to unwrap something!"

This is not how it's meant to be. The Bible is not supposed to be a parcel that only a select few get to open. It is for all of us, and every one of us should be able to unwrap at least some of its treasure.

I was heading into the thirteenth year of what would end up being a fourteen-year stint leading children's ministry at my church, and much as I loved it, I was tired. I felt like I was running the final few kilometres of a marathon and had an overwhelming desire to just stop and sit down—to be done. But the finish line was not yet in sight. There was more to complete before I could hand over the baton, and since the thought of a DNF (Did Not Finish) was unconscionable, I found myself with but one option: If I was to finish well, I would need to find my strength in God.

My love for the Bible was already firmly established. I read it often, underlining verses and writing down thoughts and ideas, sometimes embellishing them with doodles and decoration. Then one day, for reasons which I no longer recall, my doodling gave way to SOAP.

SOAP is an acronym standing for Scripture, Observation, Application and Prayer. Whilst not a new idea—I had certainly heard of it and had even used it on occasion—it was in this season of struggle that I came to fully appreciate the power of this effective Bible-reading tool.

I still remember those early days of SOAP, stretched out on my two-seater couch with a jar of stuffed olives and a kebab stick, reading my Bible and writing my SOAPs with a 2B pencil. God knew I needed it, and I'm sure He was smiling as time after time I would sit back at the end of a SOAP incredulous at what had just unfolded. God was speaking to me! He was feeding my soul and giving me strength for this race I was running.

So it was that with much relief and satisfaction, I made it to the finish line of my children's ministry service and handed over the baton. That long and wonderful race was finally over, but I've been running with SOAP ever since.

Not that SOAP is about running. In fact, the very reason SOAP is so helpful and effective in finding intimacy with God is that it requires you to stop running, and instead pause to meditate on God's inspired written Word, and to listen to the Holy Spirit. In our fast-paced 21st century life, we often don't still our minds long enough to ponder or reflect. Yet there is tremendous power in a pause. This is true for all aspects of our life, but especially for our relationship with God.

Consider the word 'meditate'. To meditate is to contemplate or consider; to focus one's mind on something; to ponder; to reflect; to mull over; to dwell on; to ruminate or chew over; to puzzle over; to turn over in one's mind. There is much value in this type of thinking and reflecting on Scripture, but it's when we invite the Holy Spirit to join us in this process that we discover intimacy with God. We're not just learning about God—we're meeting with Him.

What a remarkable blessing it is that the Holy Spirit lives in us! He is our own personal teacher, encourager, and guide, and He is the One that brings the pages of the Bible alive for us.

SOAP #6 THE QUIET PLACE

Reading: Acts 1

Scripture

In my former book, Theophilus, I wrote about all that Jesus began to do and to teach until the day he was taken up to heaven, after giving instructions through the Holy Spirit to the apostles he had chosen.

Acts 1:1-2

Observations

Even though Jesus was with His apostles in person, He gave them instructions "through the Holy Spirit." This reveals that He was 'like us' whilst on earth in the sense of operating through the Holy Spirit. He had to listen and seek the guidance of the Spirit just like I do.

Application

Jesus, You are my example of how to function whilst here in this mortal body of mine. If even You needed the Holy Spirit to guide and assist You, then I surely do too. Do You have any tips for me?

Expect Me to speak to You, and I will. Intentionally pausing to listen for My voice helps clear the airwaves of competing and confusing signals. Have confidence in what I tell you. Be humble. Set aside time. The time you spend in the quiet place is precious. It's from this pool that you draw when in 'the noisy place'. Carry the quiet place with you.

I like that. Please tell me more about the quiet place.

The quiet place is where we draw aside to speak with one another. This is the place where you draw from Me. Bring a bucket and lower it into My well of love and goodness, of wisdom and knowledge, of peace and tranquillity. Drink and reflect. The well is a place you go to, and a place you carry with you.

So, if I carry the well with me—the quiet place—I can draw from it at any moment?

Yes, for yourself, for your circumstances, and to share with others. Peace brings clarity of thought, and the ability to see more clearly.

Lord, I'm reminded of an eye. The *vitreous humor*—the clear jelly that fills the eye between the lens at the front and the retina at the back—needs to be clear so that the image reaching the back of the eye is clear. If the eye was full of 'busyness and distractions', it would be impossible to see anything clearly. In the same way, if my heart and my mind are not clear, I will find it very difficult to discern what You are saying or doing. Time in the quiet place clears the murk from my mind and my heart, enabling me to see, to discern, and to draw wisdom from You for the situation before me.

That's a nice illustration, Simon. Time with Me in the quiet place helps bring everything into focus.

Prayer

God, I look to You for wisdom and understanding, for guidance and peace. May I have a clear head and a clear heart.

SEVEN S: SCRIPTURE

So the scene is set. You're inspired, and you've secured a little pocket of time by yourself to launch into your first SOAP. You'll need a Bible, and something to write your SOAP on, such as a notebook, journal, or digital device. Write the date at the top and leave space to add a title once your SOAP is finished. If you use a digital device, you may wish to create a template to use each time.

The first letter of SOAP is S for Scripture. If you're new to the Bible or are not sure where to start reading, you'll find some helpful tips in Appendix 2 at the back of this book. Once you've decided where you're going to read, you are ready to begin.

The best way to begin is to *pause and pray*. Start well. Don't just rattle off a quick prayer. Pause. Intentionally create space to enjoy a moment of peace and stillness with God. Allow your shoulders to drop. Breathe. Relax into God. Then pray, maybe something like this: "Thank You, Lord. Thank You for Your love. Thank You that You are with me. I open my heart to You now. Please meet with me as I read. I am listening."

Now, you're ready to read.

As you read through your chosen passage of Scripture, look for something that seems to stand out to you. Or, as I like to say, "read and fish."

Allow me to explain.

When I was young, I used to go fishing from the rocky shore, or sometimes a jetty. I would cast my rod, wind in the slack, then put my finger under the line, waiting for a bite. Sometimes, I might detect a subtle nibbly feeling on the line. *Is that a fish?* I would think to myself. Other times, there'd be a sharp tug. *Yep, that's definitely a fish.* And just occasionally, the line would pull so hard, I'd know that something huge was on the line.

With SOAP, read your Bible passage just like that—like a fisherman waiting for a bite. It may be a verse, a phrase, or even just a word that tugs at you. Something you read may seem to ring a bell in your head and remind you of another Scripture or a theme you've noticed running through the Bible. It might be subtle, just a wee nibble. It might be a solid tug, or even something huge.

Whatever it is that catches your attention, that's your Scripture.

You might think to yourself, *But why this verse? Why this word? Why this thought?*

It's the Holy Spirit prompting you, drawing something to your attention. And, just like when you're fishing, you don't always know what you've hooked until it's reeled in and sitting on the jetty—in other words, until you've finished your Observations and Application.

Now sometimes when you go fishing, you cast out your line and nothing bites. It's the same when you read your Bible. You won't always have something catch your attention, so when that happens, try just moving to the observation section of your SOAP. God may well unfold something for you there. However, there are days when it seems that nothing at all is 'biting', and that's okay. Wind in your rod, relax, and relish this opportunity to just sit on the jetty and enjoy some conversation with God.

Nevertheless, be sure that you have not discounted something that the Holy Spirit has brought to your attention just because you couldn't immediately see the application. Often, the treasure He has for you is hidden, waiting to be uncovered. Imagine you're an archaeologist exploring a desert. As you walk along, your toe catches on something in the sand. You could just carry on walking, but something makes you stop. *What was that?!* It seems like just a bit of stone, but as you push away the sand, the stone starts to look more interesting. You grab a shovel and start to dig. The more you uncover, the more excited you get. "This isn't just a stone. It's the rooftop of a house! Who knows, there could be a city buried under here!"

In the same way, if your 'archaeologist's toe' seems to catch on something as you read through your Bible passage, take note. Make this Scripture the 'S' for your SOAP, even if the significance of it is not immediately apparent. Continue to read the whole passage so you have the full context, but if the Holy Spirit has drawn something to your attention, there is bound to be something hidden there just waiting to be uncovered as you move through the next two parts of your SOAP.

SOAP #7: BREATHE AND BE BREATHED UPON

Reading: Exodus 23-24

Scripture

Six days you shall do all your work, but on the seventh day do not work, so that your ox and your donkey may rest and the slave born in your household, and the alien as well, may be refreshed.

Exodus 23:12

Observations

God is concerned with our wellbeing, and so He commanded the Israelites to have rest and refreshment. This was to be for everyone, even animals, and even the ground.

In addition to a weekly rest, three times a year there were festivals which had the dual role of focusing the people on God and giving them a holiday. The sabbaths and the festivals therefore provided for physical, mental, and spiritual refreshment.

To *refresh* is: to breathe; to be breathed upon, to be refreshed (as if by a current of air).

Application

Refreshment should be a natural part of my life, a cycle, like a clock consisting of many cogs, some small, some large, and a very few larger still. As time ticks by, each cog goes through its cycle, pausing for a second to rest between each movement, or for a minute, or maybe for an hour. This is the way God plans for me to work and rest. Every part of me needs to be regularly refreshed—the physical, the mental and the spiritual. For true refreshment, all three need my disciplined attention.

Prayer

Thank You, Lord, for the opportunity to rest. Thank You for the refreshment that comes from reading and hearing Your Word, and the opportunity to pause and enjoy spending time with You. Here I am, Lord, to unwind, to worship, and to drink from Your spring of living water—to breathe and be breathed upon.

EIGHT O: OBSERVATIONS

Have you ever travelled to an unfamiliar place, perhaps even another country, and arrived in the dark? You can maybe see just a little, but until the sun comes up, you really have no idea what's outside and are reliant on what you can hear and smell to get a sense of your new surroundings.

During my final year as a medical student, I travelled to the Pacific Island nation of Vanuatu for a three-month elective. It was dark when my plane touched down in Port Vila. As I stepped out of the plane, I was hit by a wall of hot humid air laden with the smells of wet tarmac, jet fumes, and a myriad of unfamiliar tropical aromas. After navigating customs, I was met by a driver who had come to take me to the hospital where I would stay. He had a big smile, but the language barrier meant we shared little conversation as he drove me through the dark, narrow streets. It was raining, and the paucity of streetlamps gave me little clue as to my surroundings, except that there were lots of trees and lots of puddles.

It was the middle of the night when I arrived at my accommodation. There was not a soul about. I was bursting with questions and curiosity. *What's outside? What's making that strange sound? Gosh, it's hot here. Hey, look, a lizard on the wall. I wonder how far away the sea is? Are there mountains nearby? I wonder if they have snakes here? Who will I meet tomorrow? What will the food be like?*

Even in the darkness, all of my senses were on full alert as I lay on my bed waiting for the sun to rise so I could go outside to look around and explore.

That's exactly what you do in the second section of SOAP—look around, explore, and make 'Observations'. Imagine yourself waking up in the Bible passage you're reading and seeing it for the very first time. Let your senses go into overdrive as you immerse yourself in the scene, and in particular, the Scripture (your 'S') that has stood out to you. Search and examine, ponder, reflect, notice things, let your mind burst with questions and curiosity. *What do you observe? What thoughts come to mind? What stands out?* Talk with God as you go along. Trust the thoughts He gives you.

But don't just think—whatever He highlights to you, write it down. You don't need to write like a Pulitzer prize-winning author. No one's going to mark your responses—remember, you're writing for you. Your aim is simply to experience intimacy with God through the Bible, and writing will help.

Something special happens when we write things down. If all we do is sit and think, a myriad of thoughts may float through our minds but most of them will waft away in the same way that they arrived. But when we write our thoughts down, we capture them. A narrative begins, and each captured thought builds upon the last until a story unfolds.

Think of a jigsaw puzzle. Recording your thoughts is like putting the pieces of a puzzle in place. At first, they may not look like much, but soon, a picture will start to emerge. By the time you get to the end of your SOAP, you'll be astonished at what has taken shape before your eyes and what you've discovered. This is the wonder of SOAP.

Here are some guidelines to help you as you make your observations:

1. Establish the Context

One of the first things to observe is the context. Context refers to the circumstances in which your scripture is set. *What is this whole book or letter about? What was happening at that time in history or in that particular scene? Who were these words spoken to? Do they apply just to the people back then, or to me as well? How does what I am reading fit in with the overall theme of the Bible?* It is quite possible to get completely off-track if you take one sentence in isolation and ignore its context. That is *not* the purpose of SOAP. Understanding the context of the scripture God has highlighted to you will safeguard you from drawing wrong conclusions. If you're not sure, do some homework or seek advice.

2. Find the Facts

Once you've established the context, consider the facts. For example, in Genesis 22 where God asks Abraham to take his son Isaac and offer him as a sacrifice, we're told that Abraham got up early the next morning and left his home to do what God had asked him to do. So, we might observe that *Abraham didn't wait to obey God*. He did it first thing the next morning. There is no interpretation required here. It's a straightforward fact, and if it stands out to you, write it down. There is bound to be an application that follows.

3. Zoom In and Out

The story of God's plan for mankind is vast, stretching from before the beginning of time and on into eternity. But God is also interested in the small details of our lives, in what is happening right now in this moment of time. It's no surprise then that the Bible doesn't just give us the big picture, but also captures the details of the people and stories within its pages. Together they offer a wider view of God's grand plan, and how we fit into that.

So, as you mull over what you're reading, you might try zooming in for a close-up, or zooming out for a wide-angle view—or maybe both! The question is, *what is the Holy Spirit drawing you to today?* Focus your thoughts on that.

4. Look for What is Personal

Just as you'll begin to notice the big picture and the small details as you read through Scripture, you'll also find yourself making both general and personal observations. General observations either apply to everyone, or to all situations. For example, in Revelation 21:3, we read that one day, there will be a new heaven and a new earth:

> *And I heard a loud voice from the throne saying, "Now the dwelling of God is with men, and he will live with them. They will be his people, and God himself will be with them and be their God."*

Wow, one day, God is going to move in with us! Extraordinary! This is a general observation in that it applies collectively to the family of believers.

In John 14:23, on the other hand, we find a more personal observation, where Jesus says:

> *"If anyone loves me, he will obey my teaching. My Father will love him, and we will come to him and make our home with him."*

Wow, God wants to move in with me! That's equally extraordinary!

Each of these observations is a different side of the same coin, one more general, and one very personal. One is for the future, and one is for right now. Both reveal the depth of God's love for us, and how central we are in His plans.

Be sure not to miss those personal observations. The God of all mankind is also the God of you!

5. Pay Attention to the Words that Stand Out

Imagine that the verse or verses that the Holy Spirit has highlighted for you are a room.

Now, step in and have a conversation with God. "Hmm, what's in here, Lord?" As you look around, you notice a door. *That looks interesting!* So, you open it. It might turn out to be a small cupboard containing just a single item of interest. On the other hand, it might just lead into a room full of treasure! You won't know until you open it.

A word can be just like that—a doorway to something good. Let's say for example that your Scripture—the 'S' of your SOAP—is Isaiah 26:3: "You will keep in perfect peace him whose mind is steadfast, because he trusts in you." As you look at the verse, there's just something about the word 'steadfast' that appeals to you. It's like a door saying, "Open me!"

So, do it! Open it! Find out what's inside. There are two simple ways you can do this. The first is to look up the definition of the word. Yes, you read that correctly. You will be amazed at how God can speak to you from the dictionary! Just listen to some of the stirring words that define 'steadfast': *firm, determined, relentless, single-minded, staunch, loyal, faithful, devoted, reliable, dedicated, true, trusty*. Yes Lord, I want to be *all* of those words!

If the definition stirs you, write it in your SOAP. On a digital device, you can easily get a word definition by just highlighting the word and choosing 'Look Up' or 'Define' from the menu. Then if you wish you can copy and paste. Simple and quick.

Another option is to do a word search. A word search is an incredibly simple and rewarding way to explore a Bible topic and uncover hidden Bible treasure. For example, when I type 'steadfast' into the search bar in my Bible app, every Bible verse containing the word 'steadfast' appears.

This is like the jellybean trail I described earlier. I can click on the verses that grab me to see them in context and copy and paste them into my SOAP if I wish. Digital Bibles make a word search easy. But a traditional paper Bible is no barrier. You can search up a word in the concordance in the back (if it has one) or use an online resource like biblegateway.com.

Try it! Do a word search in your Bible on the word 'steadfast'. There are at least two great benefits of a word search. Firstly, it will enrich the SOAP you're presently doing. Secondly, it's an excellent way to become familiar with your Bible, since a word search can take you to parts of the Bible anywhere from Genesis to Revelation. This will add much enjoyment and value to the time you spend reading and 'SOAP-ing'.

6. Connect the Dots

It may be that as you ponder, a verse or story from another part of the Bible comes to mind. If so, look it up! Use the search function, put in two or three key words from the verse, and you'll be there.

What flavour does this 'bit on the side' add to your SOAP? Scriptures that tie in with where you're reading can throw light on your SOAP passage or bring a different angle. Nothing in the Bible stands in isolation; everything fits together like a glorious, interconnected mosaic.

For example, you might be reading in Leviticus about things that made a person clean or unclean under Old Testament Law, and as you're mulling it over, you remember the story in Mark chapter five about the woman with twelve years of menstrual bleeding. Suddenly you realise that, according to the law you're reading about in Leviticus, this woman had been 'unclean' for twelve years! For twelve years, anyone she touched in the course of a day would also have become ceremonially unclean until sundown.

No wonder she longed for healing! Not only was she physically suffering; she was effectively an outcast. This was what compelled her to creep through the crowd and touch the edge of Jesus' cloak. In theory, this should have made Jesus ceremonially unclean. Instead, she was made clean by Him, and her shame was removed forever. Joining the dots between Leviticus 15 and Mark 5 adds a whole extra layer to this story of grace.

This 'connecting of the dots' between different parts of Scripture happens more readily as you get to know the Bible more. It's one of the great blessings of reading the Bible regularly, and SOAP will help with this. So, whether you're new to the Bible or have spent a lifetime exploring it, be encouraged—the road ahead is paved with blessing, and there will always be more for you to discover.

SOAP #8: THE ULTIMATE IN DESIGNER CLOTHING

Reading: Exodus 39:1-32

Scripture

The craftsmen made beautiful sacred garments of blue, purple, and scarlet cloth—clothing for Aaron to wear while ministering in the Holy Place, just as the Lord had commanded Moses.

Exodus 39:1 NLT

Observations

Nothing unholy can stand in the presence of our holy God. In order to serve in God's presence, Aaron needed to be made holy—'sanctified' or set apart for holy service. Sacrifices needed to be made on his behalf. Not only that, but Aaron's garments also needed to be made holy by the appropriate ceremony and sacrifice. In keeping with that need for holiness, the garments were crafted from the finest fabric, colourful and richly adorned to reflect the beauty that holiness brings.

Application

I too need to be adorned in holiness if I am to enter the presence of my holy God. My old clothes are spoiled by sin and shame. Fortunately, I have some new ones!

> *I delight greatly in the Lord; my soul rejoices in my God. For he has clothed me with garments of salvation and arrayed me in a robe of righteousness.*
>
> Isaiah 61:10

My new clothes come to me at great price—Jesus, who bought them for me, was stripped of His at the cross, His garments of holiness replaced by my filthy rags in the sight of both God and man, so that I might be dressed and ready to be welcomed into the very presence of God.

I find it interesting that although His seamless "woven in one piece" undergarment was stripped from Him, it was considered too valuable to be cut in pieces. "Let's not tear it," they said to one another. "Let's decide by lot who will get it" (John 19:24). In the same way, Jesus' own holiness was not blemished or tainted at the cross. Rather, it became a precious gift—one that has somehow made its way into my hands, and to all who would humble themselves to receive it.

Prayer

Thank You, Jesus, for Your incredible gift of holiness, for these precious clothes which now adorn me and enable me to come into the presence of God, my Father. Help me, Jesus, to wear them as they should be worn, to live in holiness, and to carry myself in such a way that the giver of that holiness is recognised, praised, and acknowledged as the source of everything that is holy and good.

NINE   A: APPLICATION

I first surrendered my life to God when I was eight years old. I was at a children's camp, and I distinctly remember asking Jesus to forgive my sins and 'come into my heart'. For Jesus, the faith of a child is precious, especially that very first step, and I like to think that the angels in heaven celebrated mine that day.

I have no recollection of what happened in the years that followed that step of faith, except that at the age of fourteen, I seemed to wake from a long spiritual sleep with a growing awareness that Jesus was there—not 'in my life' as such, but rather, knocking on my door.

It felt exactly like the verse we considered earlier in Revelation 3:20 where Jesus speaks to a church and says,

> *"Here I am! I stand at the door and knock. If anyone hears my voice and opens the door, I will come in and eat with him, and he with me."*

Jesus was wooing me into a new stage of my relationship with Him, patiently and persistently knocking at my door. I knew that eventually I would have to open the door and let Him back into my life. I wanted to, but for some reason I told myself that I should put this off until I was maybe twenty-five, since by then, all the 'fun' stuff would be over.

But Jesus was very persistent, as were those who, unbeknown to me, were praying for me.

One night as I lay in bed (still aged fourteen), I could hold out no longer. "Okay Jesus," I said, "You can come in." I still remember that moment. It was as if a giant weight was lifted off my chest. That night, I willingly submitted my whole life to Jesus, once and for all.

At least, that's what I thought I was doing.

As momentous as that decision was, I have since come to realise that submission to Jesus is not just a one-time event. It's like walking; you have to keep doing it or you're no longer doing it. Though I may be filled with every good intention for the future, I cannot actually submit to Jesus in advance. Nor can I live off the devotion of my past. Submission can only happen in the present, in this moment we call 'now'—this decision, this situation, this thing God is prompting me to do. And because 'now' so quickly becomes 'then', I have to keep submitting afresh. It's like a verb in the continuous present tense: "I submit, and I keep on submitting."

But what a beautiful offering of worship that submission is. I believe that persistent, willing submission to God is the highest possible expression of our love for Him. It's for that reason that willing submission is also at the heart of SOAP.

Getting Personal

The 'Application' part of your SOAP is where you apply your observations to yourself. This is where the rubber meets the road, and the Word of God becomes God's Word to *you*. The key is submission. Genuine application begins and ends with submission.

> *"Lord, I submit myself to you. These things that I have been reading and writing and thinking about—how do they apply to me? How should I respond? What would you like me to do? What do you want me to know or learn?"*

Notice that rather than asking yourself those questions, you are asking God. *Why?* Because more than anywhere else in your SOAP, this is the moment of 'into me see', the moment you purposefully open your heart to God and seek Him. *What does God have to say? What does He want to reveal to you about Himself? Or about you?* At the very heart of SOAP are submission and obedience, and that's exactly what you are doing here—consciously submitting yourself to God, seeking His direction, and choosing to obey.

In its very essence, application is worship. But something more is happening here too. Through this act of worship, your heart is being softened and your mind is being opened, creating fertile ground for God to transform you into His likeness—in heart, in mind and in character.

This interplay between submission, worship and transformation can be seen in Romans 12:1-2 where Paul writes:

> *"Therefore, I urge you, brothers and sisters, in view of God's mercy, to offer your bodies as a living sacrifice, holy and pleasing to God—this is your true and proper worship. Do not conform to the pattern of this world, but be transformed by the renewing of your mind. Then you will be able to test and approve what God's will is—his good, pleasing and perfect will."*

It is that "good, pleasing and perfect will" that gives us such confidence to submit to God in the first place, and the more we submit, the more we are transformed so that increasingly, we find ourselves thinking and living according to the good, pleasing, and perfect will of our Father.

What sort of things might God bring to your attention as you submit yourself to Him? He may simply give you a revelation of Himself, revealing afresh some aspect of His character—His love, His faithfulness, His holiness. Enjoy this time of intimacy with Him.

The application may relate to something practical, like your relationship with a family member or work colleague. You may feel a burning desire to pray for someone at school. It may be an insight you can apply in your role at work or in your sports team. Perhaps there's an attitude God wants to help you change, or something God is encouraging you to step out and do.

Other times, God may be simply reminding you of something. *Acknowledge it and thank Him.* Or, He may be teaching you something about yourself. *Embrace it.* He may uncover some hurt in your life that He wants to heal. *Give Him permission.* Whatever comes to the surface as you do your SOAP, submit to God, and respond.

It may be that the application for your SOAP is not readily apparent, and that's okay. Just respond as seems best. It's not likely, nor is it necessary, that every SOAP will apply specifically to your current situation. Unwrapping a gift on Christmas morning doesn't mean you have to use it that afternoon, no matter how useful it is. I once bought my wife a jig saw for Christmas (the power tool, that is—not the puzzle). She loved it, and although she immediately appreciated the potential uses for this tool, she did not feel the need to carve up the Christmas ham with it.

It's the same with applying SOAP. You can appreciate the potential of what you have unwrapped even if you don't need it straight away. God is preparing you in advance, giving you tools to use in your Christian walk. Such treasures of wisdom and understanding from God accumulate, contributing to the transformation of your mind so that when the time for real-life application comes, you will know how to respond.

Let me illustrate with an example from my own life.

Our church family had embarked on a building project to enlarge our facilities and make them more useful for community work. The generosity of our small congregation enabled us to complete the work without a mortgage, which was cause for much celebration. Then, just as the work was approaching completion, a large earthquake struck our city and significantly damaged the older part of the building. Insurance covered a substantial proportion of the repair cost, but it made sense to spend a little more money to get the best value from the rebuild.

At the time, I had just read a book promoting New Testament-style house churches as a more authentic expression of church. I found myself wondering if it was right to be putting 'even more' money into this building. "After all, church is not a building," I told myself, "... it's people." I was unsettled, and as the date for our special offering approached, I started to feel a touch of resentment. Now resentment and peace cannot reside in the same room, and I certainly knew which one I wanted. The accumulated wisdom from all those SOAPs had woven itself into the fabric of my being, and now it was time to apply it.

This was my moment to submit. So, I prayed: "God, I'm Yours, and so is my money. This is Your church, and I'm in Your hands to serve however and wherever You wish. How much would You like me to give for this offering?" Straight away, a figure came into my head, and the moment I determined to give that amount, the resentment I had felt vanished and was replaced with contentment and peace. The building was completed, once more without a mortgage, and I felt free again to serve wholeheartedly in the church I had grown up in.

When You Apply, Use The Word 'I'

Now, because 'Application' is about exploring how what you have gleaned from your reading applies to you, it's important that you get personal and specific during this step. And I want to offer you a top tip to help you do that: When you apply, use the word 'I'.

I can't emphasise enough how powerful this simple rule is. Using 'I' instead of 'we' will ensure you get the best possible value from SOAP. So that you can see what I mean, let's compare the following three statements:

- *We can trust God to supply our needs.*
- *I can trust God to supply my needs.*
- *I trust You, Lord, to supply my needs.*

The first statement uses the word 'we'. As a general statement, it is true. But somehow, applying it to yourself using the word 'we' doesn't quite hit home. It's possible to accept that the statement is true without really owning it for yourself.

The second statement uses the word 'I'. Just feel the difference as you change from 'we' to 'I'. Say it out loud: "I can trust God to supply my needs!" The statement has become transformed into a personal declaration, and as you speak it out, you feel like you're nailing your colours to the mast. "Yes! I *can* trust God to supply my needs!"

The third statement then becomes the perfect response to the second. Given that you're in conversation with God through all of this, it's only natural to turn it into a prayer: "I trust You, Lord, to supply my needs."

Do you see the difference that 'I' makes? Personalising it brings the application to life.

Now it's true that sometimes it is appropriate to use the words 'we' or 'us'. For example, when we're speaking about the body of Christ, or about things we do together, of course it is important to use words like 'we' or 'us'. Just be conscious that you're doing it, and make sure you return afterwards to your default setting: *When you apply, use the word 'I'*.

The application part of your SOAP really is where we move from simply being hearers of the Word to doers of it (James 1:22-25). This is a wonderful opportunity to express your love and devotion to God through personal submission and obedience, and ultimately to connect more intimately with Him.

SOAP #9: WHEN THE DAM BREAKS

Reading: Genesis 44-45

Scripture

Then Joseph could no longer control himself before all his attendants, and he cried out, "Have everyone leave my presence!" So there was no one with Joseph when he made himself known to his brothers. And he wept so loudly that the Egyptians heard him, and Pharaoh's household heard about it . . . And he kissed all his brothers and wept over them. Afterward his brothers talked with him.

Genesis 45:1-2,15

Observations

When a dam breaks, the sudden flow of water is massive and unstoppable. If you try to stop it, you will be washed away. But if you stand aside and wait, all that pent-up water will be released, and the flow will settle.

When Joseph's dam broke, emotion burst forth like a flood. His brothers were stunned, but soon enough the strength of his emotion subsided, allowing conversation to flow like a stream running over many stones.

Application

When emotion bursts forth like a flood, I'm best not to stand in its way. Sometimes, hurt people hurt people. Rather than be offended, I should allow it to pass and wait patiently for the more gentle conversation that will hopefully follow.

It's better when things aren't allowed to build up—in myself, in my relationships, with friends or colleagues—lest the breaking of the dam brings carnage to those downstream.

Prayer

Help me, Lord, to be sensitive to people, to provide them a 'spillway' to release emotion, to be patient when dams burst, and to be there for the conversation that follows.

TEN P: PRAYER

It was 1991. I was newly engaged to be married, but for three months found myself 'otherwise engaged' in the South Pacific island nation of Vanuatu. My fiancé, meanwhile, was having her own cultural experience working in a small village on the slopes of Mt Kenya in East Africa. I thought about her every day, but I couldn't talk to her. Telephone communication between those remote places had proved impossible, and email and text had yet to be invented. So I wrote to her. It took about two weeks for each of my letters to reach her, and then two more for her reply, so we both wrote regularly, knowing that if we sent a letter today, it would effectively take four weeks to receive a response. Every day I would eagerly check the mail to see if a letter had arrived. We each longed for the day when once again we would be together, and communication would happen in real time.

And yet, there was something special about those letters, both in the writing of them and in the receiving. Although less immediate and spontaneous than speaking, the written word allowed each of us time to think and craft what we would say, and to reread and savour what the other had written.

In a sense, the unified collection of inspired writings that we call the Bible is a 'letter' to us from God—His written word, thought about and crafted so that we might have opportunity not just to hear what He has to say, but to reread and savour it. But unlike the situation with my fiancé and I, through the Holy Spirit we also have opportunity to hear God's spoken word—His voice—coming to us in real time as we read, bringing to life what is written.

Without God's spoken word, the Bible has no power to change us. We need to be able to hear God's voice as we read. We need the Spirit of God to illuminate His Word to us and empower us to respond. Neither information nor academic study are enough.

The Pharisees of Jesus' day read the Scriptures religiously yet failed to hear God's voice in them, so that when Jesus arrived—the very One of whom the Scriptures speak—they did not recognise Him.

For the psalmist David, hearing God's voice was a matter of life and death. In Psalm 28, he says,

> *"For if you remain silent, I will be like those who have gone down to the pit."* (v. 1)

In other words, *If I don't hear your voice, I might as well be dead.* It's not enough just to be able to talk to God, or even to know that He's listening. We need Him to speak to us. We need to hear His voice.

This book is about intimacy with God and how to find it, and it should be obvious that intimacy requires communication. At some level we need to be able to hear God's voice, both as we meet with Him in the Bible and as we engage with Him in prayer. So as we shift our focus now to prayer, the 'P' in SOAP, I want to suggest two forms of prayer that not only work very naturally with SOAP, but which help to nurture that two-way communication with God that we all long for. They are conversational prayer, and the prayer of response.

Conversational Prayer

For most of my life, prayer was largely a one-way affair—from me to God. But something unexpected and rather wonderful happened to me after completing the first draft of this book. I discovered there was a chapter missing, not only from the manuscript, but also from my life.

Instead of a rich, full chapter on prayer, I had only a few short paragraphs, and although they certainly carried weight, something was missing. I realised I didn't want to spend my life just talking *to* God—I wanted to talk *with* Him. I wanted a two-way conversation.

So, I paused—and in the midst of the pause, I came across what was, for me, the missing ingredient: conversational prayer. I discovered what many others had already discovered before me—that I could have a conversation with God. This practice has been momentous for me, adding much depth to my relationship with God and also to my SOAPs. Conversational prayer is a natural partner for SOAP, since both involve listening to God and writing down what He says. Conversational prayer assumes that God is able and willing to speak to us, that He is in fact speaking to us (more often than we recognise), and that it is possible to have a 'back and forth' conversation with Him. Mostly, conversations with God happen in our thoughts, and the easiest way to learn conversational prayer is to write the conversation down.

In describing how this works, allow me first to ask you a question: *How did you learn to pray?*

The Bible has a lot to say about prayer, but if you're like me, the way you pray is probably similar to what you 'grew up with' as a new believer. Like children, we watch others and copy them. Once our prayer style is learnt, we generally stick with it. Consistency is usually a good thing, but sometimes, ingrained habits can prevent us from considering new things, even things that hold the potential to be helpful or good.

Conversational prayer is not something I grew up with, but it has proved for me to be both helpful and good. I feel a deepened sense of friendship with God. I talk through things with God now, like decisions I'm making, or situations I'm grappling with. If I'm preparing a message or presentation, I ask Him for help and am amazed at the fresh wisdom and insight He gives me as we talk. I ask God questions, and sometimes He asks me a question. I often talk with God about something beautiful that has caught my eye, since He loves what He has made even more than I do!

For each of us, a conversation with God will sound different, and every conversation will have its own flavour. By way of example, here is a conversation I had with God while I was writing this chapter:

Good evening, Father.

Good evening, Simon. How is your writing going?

Slowly. It seems there is much to say and learn about conversational prayer, though it's actually easier to do than it is to write about! Can You help me bring it down to its essence?

The essence of speaking with Me is your heart. Let Me have all of it! Don't get hung up on the words you're writing or whether you've got things exactly right—just write. What's really important is not so much the words you're writing but the completeness of your submission to Me. Do you remember the way that Jesus submitted to Me?

Yes. Jesus submitted everything. He put Himself completely in Your hands. His obedience to You at the cross was the ultimate expression of love, not just love for us—for me—but love for You.

Yes, you see it, Simon. Willing submission is the ultimate act of love. So let submission to Me be at the heart of your prayers and at the centre of our conversations. As Jesus submitted to Me, you submit to Me too—He is your mentor. And when this attitude becomes the foundation of our conversations, the words will flow.

Lord, when I first started with this way of talking with You, I felt almost immediately a new sense of friendship between us, as if a whole other dimension to our relationship had opened up. I was almost a little afraid that this new familiarity might lead to over-familiarity on my part; that is, that I might unintentionally slip into talking with You as if You were an equal rather than the awesome, holy, creator God. (Just the thought of this makes me wince).

What does the word 'familiarity' mean? Look it up.

Familiarity: acquaintance with, informality, casualness, ease, comfortableness, friendliness, lack of ceremony, lack of restraint, lack of reserve, naturalness, simplicity.

Do you think it is possible to have intimacy with Me—to 'into me see'—without familiarity?

No, I don't imagine it is.

There is that saying, "familiarity breeds contempt"—perhaps you had that in your mind—but familiarity doesn't have to breed contempt. Lack of ceremony does not have to mean lack of respect. Lack of reserve does not have to mean you're overstepping the mark. In fact, reserve must be put aside if true intimacy is to occur. Another word to consider, Simon, is 'honour'. Within the Godhead, we honour one another. It's the 'family way'. So now that you are in the family, you should bring that same attitude into our conversations, as in fact you are. Again, it's your heart that's important.

Lord, I often think of Lucy in the Narnia series by C.S. Lewis. She had such a wonderful freedom and closeness with Aslan. She came to him with the sort of childlike innocence that I think You want me to come to You with. When I think of her, I think of what You said, Jesus: "Blessed are the pure in heart, for they shall see God." It makes me want to be pure like that.

Simon, You can have that same relationship with Me. True friendship with Me always leads to holiness, and within the boundaries of holiness, there is much freedom. So come and speak freely with Me, and let our conversations bring a new closeness in our relationship.

Thank You, Lord. They already are!

This was such a helpful conversation for me. It shifted my focus away from the 'how to' of conversational prayer and onto the heart of it—my attitude. Humility, submission, a desire to honour God—these are the essence of my relationship with God, and 'nuts and bolts' should not distract me from that. Nonetheless, nuts and bolts do help to hold things together. And so, in addition to what came out in that conversation I had with God, I would like to share some keys that might help you too.

1. Exercise Faith

Every aspect of our relationship with God requires faith, and hearing God's voice is no different. You can't learn to walk on water by staying in your boat. Sooner or later, like Peter, you're going to have to get out of your boat and walk. In the case of conversational prayer, that means you're going to have to trust God and write down the words that come into your mind, even if you're not sure. With time, distinguishing God's voice will become easier, but it will always require faith.

2. Relax and Write

Bible translators invest countless hours fastidiously and meticulously translating ancient Scriptures into modern-day English. That's not what you're doing here. Rather, you're like a novice interpreter listening to a conversation and quickly transcribing as you go, using your own vocabulary and doing the best you can. You are not writing the Bible—you are learning to listen to God's voice, and writing it down helps. So, relax and write.

3. Come as a Child

When adults are learning to speak a new language, they are often self-conscious and afraid of making mistakes or getting it wrong. Infants and young children have no such reservations. They happily try out new words or phrases, and they don't at all mind being corrected—they are blissfully unconcerned about getting it wrong on their way to getting it right.

So, when it comes to hearing God's voice, come as a child. Discern God's voice as best you can, and exercise patience as you learn and grow. It's unlikely that any of us will get it right one hundred percent of the time whilst we walk on this earth, but that should not stop us from trying. What it should do is stop us from being dogmatic and thinking we are always correct.

Humility is a wonderful thing. It frees us to admit we got something wrong whilst affording maximum opportunity to learn from God. And we learn best when we come to Him as a child.

4. Let God be God

Our hopes and expectations of God should always be tempered by the knowledge that God's ways are best.

When we're in need of guidance and ask, "Lord, what should I do in this situation?" we're usually hoping for an immediate and straightforward answer, but instead of an answer, God in His wisdom will often engage us in a conversation. And while God does sometimes give immediate answers, it seems He is never in a hurry—He is more concerned about the process than the outcome, because it's in the process that we grow and mature. Like it or not, a conversation can at times be more helpful than a direct answer.

For example, God wants me to grow in wisdom, and He promises in James chapter one that if anyone asks for wisdom and does not doubt, He will receive it. Wisdom is the ability to weigh up and carefully consider all the facts, and then arrive at a good decision. So, when God gives wisdom, He usually also provides the opportunity to exercise it. Were God to immediately answer all my questions in a quick conversation, I would not need to exercise wisdom, so I would never grow wise.

Instead, God often gives me the opportunity to find my own way through (or so it seems) by exercising the wisdom He has given me, and when I look back, I can see how He has been at work both in the situation and in me. My point is this: if a straightforward answer from God is not forthcoming in your conversation with Him, don't be disheartened. Keep talking, keep trusting, and let God be God.

5. Keep the Bible in its Rightful Place

Let's make one thing clear: the Bible is our final authority. So, if you find that the content of your conversation with God seems at odds with truth as revealed in Scripture, put aside your conversation and humbly accept what the Bible teaches. God will never contradict what He has already made clear in His inspired written Word.

Like guard rails, the Scriptures help us stay in the right lane and avoid error. They are a lamp to our feet and a light for our path (Psalm 119:105), and though conversational prayer can be a great blessing, it can never replace hearing God's voice through the Scriptures. So, as you enjoy conversing with God, be sure to keep the Bible in its rightful place.

Using Conversational Prayer with SOAP

Conversational prayer can be used wherever it seems natural to use it. Obviously, you can use it as your final prayer of response, but you can also launch into conversation anytime during your SOAP. I find it works particularly well with the *application*. For example, you might start your application with, "Lord, how does this apply to me?" or, "God, here's what I'm thinking…" and away you go. You're still following the standard SOAP format, but the result can sometimes be sharper and more specific when you include a conversation.

You will discover that SOAP and conversational prayer mutually benefit one another. While the latter can help you to hear God's voice more clearly as you do your SOAP, increasing familiarity with the Scriptures can help to keep your prayer conversations grounded. As already alluded to, you're less likely to get funny ideas in your head if your head is full of the Word. Moreover, God will readily bring Scriptures to mind as you talk with Him, bringing richness and weight to your conversations.

Whether you are listening for God's voice though Scripture or through prayer, you are listening for one and the same voice. Jesus said, "My sheep listen to my voice" (John 10:27). So, Lord, soften our hearts to hear Your voice and respond.

The Prayer of Response

Having opened your heart to God, read from the Bible, and spent time thinking, writing and talking with God, the time comes to bring your SOAP to a conclusion with a final prayer of response. This prayer can be as long or as short as you like because in a sense, the whole SOAP has been a form of prayer. You have listened to God and responded, and these are your final words. I am reminded of what Jesus said:

"For out of the overflow of the heart the mouth speaks."
Matthew 12:34

This final prayer will likely be just that—your overflow—a written expression of whatever is welling up within you. It might also include a commitment, a request, a declaration, or simply an expression of gratitude and trust. Whatever it is that has come up during your time with God, encapsulate it in this prayer of response.

Of course, what's really important is not so much the prayer you write, but the posture of your heart. When you respond to Him with trust and humility and obedience, God receives it as a most beautiful expression of devotion and worship.

In Genesis 47, Jacob (aka Israel) had come to the end of his life. His affairs were finally in order, all the boxes were ticked, and he could now rest. Verse 31 records that "Israel bowed in worship at the head of his bed" (NASB). Or, as some versions translate it, "as he leaned on the top of his staff." In response to all that had happened, Jacob took this moment to express his deep gratitude and reverence to God.

So as you finish your SOAP, why not also take a moment to 'lean on the top of your staff' and worship.

Reading: Luke 1

SOAP #10
GRACE IS THE ANTIDOTE TO DISGRACE

Scripture

When Zechariah's time of service was completed, he returned home. After this his wife Elizabeth became pregnant and for five months remained in seclusion. "The Lord has done this for me," she said. "In these days he has shown his favour and taken away my disgrace among the people."

Luke 1:23-25

Observations

Luke chapter one must be one of the most 'feel-good' chapters in the Bible. I love the story of Zechariah and Elizabeth.

Both of them were upright in the sight of God, observing all the Lord's commandments and regulations blamelessly. But they had no children, because Elizabeth was barren; and they were both well along in years.

Luke 1:6-7

Through no fault of her own, Elizabeth lived in disgrace among the people because of her barrenness.

'Disgrace' refers to: a loss of reputation or respect as a result of a dishonourable action; a person or thing regarded as shameful and unacceptable; loss of honour or esteem; ignominy; shame; public contempt.

How much pain must Elizabeth have carried in her heart, along with her husband Zechariah. Yet the two of them continued to serve God and do their best to please Him.

And then, inexplicably and against all the odds, Elizabeth learns she has been chosen to bear a son! He will be called John. "He will be a joy and delight to you, and many will rejoice because of his birth, for he will be great in the sight of the Lord" (Luke 1:14-15). Elizabeth must have nearly burst with happiness as her 'dis-grace' vanished like the morning dew. The 'dis-' was gone forever, leaving her to enjoy what God had for her all along: "—grace".

Application

No matter how much 'dis-' there has been in my life, whether inflicted by others or the result of my own actions, Jesus has taken it to the cross. He carried it in His body to the grave and it is gone forever, leaving me to enjoy what God had for me all along—grace.

Grace and disgrace cannot coexist. They are opposites. A person cannot truly experience God's grace (that is, His undeserved favour), and still be weighed down by shame and condemnation.

Grace is the antidote to disgrace.

The coming of grace is like the rising of the sun, causing disgrace to vanish like the morning dew.

This is my mission as a follower of Jesus—to bring grace. What an exciting and rewarding prospect, to have the Holy Spirit working not just in me but through me to bring the wonderful love and favour of God to all who would receive it.

Prayer

Father, let me be a channel for Your grace! May it flow through me like an ever-increasing river. Help me to use my gifts and to take every opportunity You give me to share Your grace, and to bring joy where there was despair.

> *Each one should use whatever gift he has received to serve others, faithfully administering God's grace in its various forms.*
>
> 1 Peter 4:10

ELEVEN TAKING SOAP FURTHER

Once you have completed the four steps of SOAP, there are some final touches and complementary practices you may want to add to the mix to really enhance your time with God in the Bible, and to keep it fresh and vibrant.

Add the Final Touches

1. Give Your SOAP a Title

It makes good sense to round off each SOAP by adding a title. A title should capture the essence of your SOAP so that when you're looking back over your collection, you'll know what each SOAP is about, and will more easily be able to track down one you're looking for. On a digital device, a quick search will readily bring up all the titles containing the key word.

Assigning tags or topic categories to each SOAP will make it even easier to bring up everything on a particular theme. You can usually assign as many tags or categories to a document as you wish, and being able to look back over your growing collection of SOAPs and see all that God has taught you about a certain topic or theme will make your SOAPs a valuable personal resource.

2. Add Some Artistry

Now this is definitely an optional extra, but I personally enjoy making my SOAPs look nice. Photography is my thing, and because I do SOAP on an iPad, it's very easy to insert a choice photo. This serves two purposes. Firstly, it makes each SOAP more visually appealing. Secondly, it gives each SOAP a unique look, which helps me remember it in my mind's eye and find it again if other search methods have failed. I also enjoy an interesting font or two, and have set up a little template to write my SOAPs on. So, if you are wired on the arty side, feel free to add your own flair and give your SOAPs a touch of the creative. Alternatively, you might like to write your SOAPs by hand in a lovely journal.

Whatever your style, make it yours. Remember, in writing these SOAPs, you are creating a personal record of your dealings with God. Some of these will be quite special—you may find yourself coming back to them many times over the years ahead, or even sharing the odd one, so a little decoration is a nice touch if you are so inclined.

Go a Little Deeper on a Topic

Often as you read the Bible, something will grab your attention and set you off on a 'rabbit trail' of sorts. It may be a topic or an idea you'd like to explore. Perhaps there's a word you have a hankering to trace through Scripture, or a person you'd like to know more about. Don't be afraid to study beyond the basic SOAP outline. If your curiosity is piqued or a question has popped into your mind, explore it! For example:

- *What is glory?*
- *What does the New Testament have to say about giving?*
- *Mary is such an inspiring woman—what else can I find out about her?*
- *What will happen in the end times?*
- *What did the writer have in mind when they used the phrase, "the word of God"?*
- *I'd like to understand more about the sabbath.*

The list of potential topics is endless. So, pay attention to the Holy Spirit's promptings and if something piques your interest, go deeper. Mostly, you can do this without even leaving your Bible. Use some of the tools mentioned earlier. Read around the verses for more context.

And ask the Holy Spirit for understanding. Almost invariably, if He highlights a topic for you, there will be treasure to find.

Once you have examined a topic yourself, you might consider exploring what others have said about it. Commentaries and Bible dictionaries can shed light on cultural aspects of what you are reading, add context, or identify themes that you may have missed. Online resources such as the Bible Project use videos and podcasts to explore biblical themes and provide both overviews and in-depth studies which can certainly broaden your understanding and appreciation of the Bible. Just make sure you continue to sharpen your own skills, and remember, the Holy Spirit is not just a wonderful teacher—He is *your* teacher.

SOAP # 11
SELF-TALK: THE POWER OF LIFE AND DEATH

Reading: Lamentations 1-5

Scripture

"I remember my affliction and my wandering, the bitterness and the gall. I well remember them, and my soul is downcast within me. Yet this I call to mind and therefore I have hope: Because of the Lord's great love we are not consumed, for his compassions never fail. They are new every morning; great is your faithfulness. I say to myself, 'The Lord is my portion; therefore I will wait for him.'"

Lamentations 3:19-24

Observations

It is often said that talking to yourself is the first sign of madness. But here in Lamentations, in the midst of difficulty and affliction, Jeremiah is doing just that—talking to himself.

It's as if the part of him that speaks and directs is able somehow to separate itself from the circumstances of his physical body and then, from that removed position, encourage and direct the rest of his being.

Like 'time out' in a sports match, Jeremiah gathers himself to recall, to remind, to refocus, and ultimately to rekindle his faith in God's unchanging love. He knows what is true, so he speaks it out, to himself.

Application

That voice that God has given me—the one I use to talk to myself—it has power! Just as Jeremiah and the psalmists and numerous other Bible characters talked themselves through doubt and difficulty, so I can keep myself on track by speaking to myself truth and self-encouragement.

Proverbs 18:21 says, "The tongue has the power of life and death." So when it comes to speaking to myself, I need to speak life!

I can make declarations based on Scripture, and statements born from faith. I can instruct myself according to what I know from the Bible.

In Ephesians 4:29, Paul says, "Do not let any unwholesome talk come out of your mouths, but only what is helpful for building others up according to their needs, that it may benefit those who listen." It hasn't occurred to me before, but this principle applies just as much to the way I talk to myself as it does to the way I talk to others!

Negative self-talk should never cross my lips. It only gives the devil a foothold to accuse and discourage me. Nor should feelings or circumstances determine how I talk to myself, since they so easily change. Truth, on the other hand, is solid and unchanging. What do I know about God? What does God say about me? These things I can declare.

All this serves to remind me how vital it is that I read my Bible and declare it with my mouth and keep on declaring it. As I speak and declare to myself the truths in God's Word, my faith will grow, my confidence will rise, and with God's help I will achieve all the plans and purposes that He has for my life.

Prayer

Lord God, You are so good. Everything You do is perfect. Thank You for Your written Word, and for the voice of Your ever-present Holy Spirit. I offer to You now my own voice and pray that just as You purified Isaiah's lips with a coal from Your altar, You will purify mine. May they always only ever speak life, both to me and to others.

"Praise the Lord, my soul; all my inmost being, praise his holy name."

Psalm 103:1

TWELVE COMPLEMENTING SOAP

One of the best ways to complement your time with God in the Bible is to memorise Scripture.

Memorising Scripture is a wonderfully helpful discipline. Every verse you memorise is a tool added to your spiritual tool kit. This tool kit is not just yours; you share it with the Holy Spirit. As you work side by side with the Spirit in your everyday life, He helps you to use the tools in your tool kit, bringing a dimension of effectiveness that is beyond your natural ability. Spiritual gifts are one type of tool. Memorised verses are another.

The Holy Spirit can use the verses we memorise to encourage and guide us, and to give us strength and wisdom in a moment of need. He can also help us use those same verses to build up and encourage others, so that the benefit is shared. Memorised verses will also frequently come to mind during our time in the Bible, shedding light on what we are currently reading and helping us to connect one part of the Bible's story with another.

My father was passionate about birds. At home we had many books about New Zealand native birds, and when walking through a forest or a wetland, or along a beach, we always took pleasure in trying to identify the different bird calls we heard along the way. I remember my dad and I climbing into a rata tree on Stewart Island with a tape recorder to capture the wonderful birdsong of tui feeding on the deep red flowers.

Every Bible verse you memorise is like a bird with a unique call. As you walk through your day, as you talk with people, as you pray, as you read your Bible, suddenly a verse will pop into your mind, like a tui breaking into song, or a fantail cheerfully announcing its presence, or a paradise duck sounding the alarm. Each memorised verse has its own sound, its own purpose, its own opportunity to reveal its beauty.

Imagine a forest with no birdsong, or a landscape that has lost its wildlife. Your mind needn't be like that. Populate it with even a few favourite verses, and when the moment comes, one of them will burst into song like the very first bird at the break of dawn.

Which verses should you memorise? Start with the ones you like, and the ones you think will be helpful. Be sure to include verses that have impacted you, that contain promises from God, and that encapsulate important truths. Try writing the verse and its reference onto a card and putting it somewhere you'll see it often. Children's Bible songs are also a surprisingly good way to learn verses. Memorising Scripture—however you go about it—is a wonderfully worthwhile discipline, which I heartily commend to you.

SOAP #12 THE COLOUR OF HEAVEN

One morning recently, in that dreamy place between fully asleep and fully awake, something I had read in the past about flamingos and salmon floated into my head. Here are the 'ponderings' that followed. You'll notice I substituted the S for Scripture to 'Something God Has Created':

Something God Has Created

Salmon and Flamingos

Observations

Flamingos and salmon have something in common—their colour is determined by what they eat.

For flamingos, it's blue-green algae, or the shrimps which feed on those algae. The algae contain carotenoids which, after being consumed, are broken down into colourful pigments and deposited in the feathers, legs and beak, giving flamingos their characteristic pink or sometimes orange colour.

Likewise, salmon absorb the same colourful pigments from the krill and shrimps they eat. Salmon raised in farms have to have the pigment added to their diet, or their flesh would be its natural colour, grey.

In the case of the flamingo, what it has been eating is obvious from the outside, whereas the salmon hides its colour under silvery skin. But underneath, it is 'salmon-coloured' to the core.

Application

I am what I eat, and not just in the sense of physical food. The things I dwell on colour my thinking—what I read, what I watch, what I listen to, who I listen to. What I consume has the power to change me!

But I am not just what I consume. My thinking is also coloured by what I dwell on. If I persistently dwell on my fears, anxiety will colour my thinking right to the core. On the other hand, if I dwell on God's love for me, or look for beauty in His creation or in the people I meet, the natural colour of my inner being will be a far more pleasant hue.

This reminds me of Paul's advice in Philippians:

> *Finally, brothers, whatever is true, whatever is noble, whatever is right, whatever is pure, whatever is lovely, whatever is admirable—if anything is excellent or praiseworthy—think about such things.*
> *Philippians 4:8*

There is another side to this. I have the opportunity not just to absorb the pigment of life myself, but to share it. My words have the potential to colour people's thinking about themselves, their situation, and their value as a person, shifting their perhaps naturally grey hue a shade closer to the 'colour of heaven'.

Prayer

I like this illustration, Lord. I want You to colour my thinking. If there is any colour in me that's not from Your colour palette, please remove it and replace it with something more pleasing. May my thoughts be the colour of heaven right to the core, and my words bring Your colour to others.

THIRTEEN: SOAP IS FOR SHARING

The primary purpose of SOAP is to feed yourself and enjoy intimacy with God. The moment it stops being about that, you will lose its foremost blessing. But inevitably, there will be times when you get to the end of a SOAP, and think, "Wow! That is *so* good!" And you'll want to share it. Not only that, but SOAP can be a great source of mutual blessing when you do it with others. Let's explore the ways you can share SOAP.

Sharing Your SOAPs with Others

Although some SOAPs are very personal and unique to you, others will be more generally applicable, and therefore suitable for sharing.

You can share a SOAP with an individual or with a wider audience, in person or in writing. As you finish a SOAP, or are looking back on some older ones, God may put a particular person on your heart to share that SOAP with. Let the Holy Spirit be your guide. In the same way that He prompts us to phone someone or pray for them or take them some produce from the garden, He can prompt us to share with them a particular SOAP. Who knows how timely that word in season might turn out to be.

Like apples of gold in settings of silver is a word spoken in right circumstances.
                          Proverbs 25:11, NASB

So long as you use discretion and are motivated by love, your overflow can be like honey dew, "sweet to the soul and healing to the bones" (Proverbs 16:24).

SOAP In Your Small Group

SOAP and small groups were made for each other! There are two ways you can use SOAP in your small group.

Firstly, individual members can share a SOAP with the group. Sharing fresh revelation from God can be very encouraging, and people who 'SOAP' invariably have something to share. A good SOAP can spark much discussion, and if SOAP is the norm for your group members, your meetings will never be short of something to talk about!

Secondly, you can do a SOAP together. Choose one passage of Scripture and do one of two things: Give the group the passage ahead of time so they can do a SOAP before the meeting; or, set aside 15-20 minutes of quietness during the meeting for each person to do a short SOAP. Then allow all who want to share their SOAP to do so. Depending on the size of your gathering, you might also take a short moment after each person's SOAP to respond with prayer for the person, or with praise to God.

Just about any passage of Scripture can be used for SOAP in a group. Narrative or story-based passages work particularly well. You will be amazed at how God can have so many different things to say through the same passage! Everyone brings their own experience, and their own perspective. The collective word that results is rich and full.

This is how a small group should operate, with the Holy Spirit having full reign to speak and work through every member of the group. Having everyone contribute takes the onus off the leader to be the 'oracle' to whom everyone looks. Instead, the load is spread, and the leader's preparation time is reduced. Not only does this make small group leadership more doable, but the whole group matures as each one 'grows into' their place in the Body of Christ.

I have been using the term 'small group' to describe what you might know as a home group, a life group, a cell group or a connect group. However, the smallest 'small group' might simply be two people who get together for the express purpose of reading the Bible together, doing a SOAP, and sharing with each other what God has given them. What a wonderful basis for a friendship. God bless you as you share His goodness with others!

Let the word of Christ dwell in you richly as you teach and admonish one another with all wisdom, and as you sing psalms, hymns and spiritual songs with gratitude in your hearts to God.
Colossians 3:16

SOAP #13 A GENTLE AND HUMBLE HEART

Reading: Matthew 11

Scripture

Come to me, all you who are weary and burdened, and I will give you rest. Take my yoke upon you and learn from me, for I am gentle and humble in heart, and you will find rest for your souls. For my yoke is easy and my burden is light.

Matthew 11:28-30

Observations

I love the joy in Jesus' voice as He says these words. You can hear it welling up in Him as he speaks. It's what immediately precedes His invitation that gives us this insight—it was a lament. So many in that generation had seen His miracles and heard His proclamations yet had failed to respond to Him. Their hearts were hard. Here's a taste:

Woe to you, Korazin! Woe to you, Bethsaida! If the miracles that were performed in you had been performed in Tyre and Sidon, they would have repented long ago in sackcloth and ashes.

Matthew 11:21

The frustration is evident in the tone of His voice. Frustration, and sadness. But then, suddenly, it happens—a glorious shift in His thoughts, away from those who have scorned Him and onto those who, with childlike faith, have welcomed Him. The emotions come rolling in like a wave and lift Him up with joy and love and compassion.

> *At that time Jesus said, "I praise you, Father, Lord of heaven and earth, because you have hidden these things from the wise and learned, and revealed them to little children. Yes, Father, for this was your good pleasure."*
>
> Matthew 11:25-26

This is the moment when, filled with compassion and love, He makes His heartfelt invitation:

> *Come to me, all you who are weary and burdened, and I will give you rest.*
>
> Matthew 11:28

Application

Jesus' invitation is to the 'little children' to whom, for His good pleasure, God has revealed the glorious truth about His Son. The simple childlike hope I place in Jesus fills Him with delight. He reaches out to me! He reassures me! "I am gentle and humble in heart." "Learn from me!" "Let your heavy burdens go." "Come alongside me and I'll teach you how to live in the warmth of the Father's good pleasure." Why wouldn't I want to live like that?!

> Jesus, does pride or conceit still have any foothold in my heart? What am I carrying? What burdens can I put down right now? How can I free my heart to fully embrace your heartfelt invitation?
>
> *Do you trust me, Simon? Do you believe that I'm working for your good? Do you believe that I can meet all your needs and that I will always have your best at heart?*
>
> Yes Jesus, I do.
>
> *Then rest, and let your confidence be in me, for this is my Father's good pleasure.*

Prayer

Thank You, Jesus, for Your invitation. I want to walk alongside You, to be yoked with You, and to learn from You with each step of my life the attitudes and practices of a gentle and humble heart.

FOURTEEN: OTHER WAYS TO SOAP

So far, we have focused on finding intimacy with God through the Scriptures, but the Observation, Application and Prayer principles used in SOAP can also be helpful in other contexts, especially hearing God's voice through creation.

In Psalm 19:1-4, the psalmist tells us:

The heavens declare the glory of God; the skies proclaim the work of his hands. Day after day they pour forth speech; night after night they display knowledge. There is no speech or language where their voice is not heard. Their voice goes out into all the earth, their words to the ends of the world.

Observing Creation

There is so much we can learn about God by observing the things He has made. Even in its now less-than-perfect state, God's creation is full of beauty and brimming with lessons. As Paul said,

". . . since the creation of the world God's invisible qualities—his eternal power and divine nature—have been clearly seen, being understood from what has been made, so that men are without excuse."

Romans 1:20

Everything we see and everything we have, came into being because God spoke. He spoke and the world was created. He spoke and our faith was born. Even now, He speaks, and our needs are provided for. Our ability to work exists because He ordained it. He is our Source. We live by everything that proceeds from the mouth of God. We can also *learn* from everything that proceeds from the mouth of God. In just the same way that God speaks to us through what was *written* by the word of His mouth, He can speak to us through what was *created* by the word of His mouth.

To hear God speaking to us through His creation, all we need is the same open, teachable heart that we bring when we read the Bible. A rosebud opening up might speak to us of potential, or of being the aroma of Christ. A hermit crab might challenge us to take courage and leave our small limiting shell for a bigger one. A tiny flower might reveal the beauty hidden in small things, like small beginnings, or small acts of kindness. A spider building its web might inspire us to be diligent and patient, and a forest ecosystem might remind us of the benefit of cooperation and of nurturing one another for the common good.

Once you get started, you can see it everywhere—like treasure just waiting to be discovered. Truly, the world that God has made is a repository for vast amounts of wisdom. If you open your eyes and open your heart, God will speak.

You can add even more value to your observations in nature by writing a SOAP to help you reflect. Instead of 'S' being for Scripture, begin with 'S' for: *Something God Has Made.*

Then simply proceed with your observations, your application, and your prayer. Easy! And don't forget, *when you apply, use the word 'I'.*

Observing Other Things

Just as He speaks though the Scriptures and creation, God can also draw your attention to other things in your world. A photograph. A situation you observe. An item in the news. If something seems to stand out to you, ask the question, "Lord, is there something you want to say to me through this?"

Here, the 'S' for your SOAP could stand for 'Something that has caught my attention' or, 'Something that has delighted me', or even 'Something that has disturbed me'. Again, simply write it down, apply SOAP, and see what unfolds. This is the beauty of SOAP. It teaches you to listen and reflect. After a while, listening to the voice of the Holy Spirit becomes second nature, and you find yourself 'always on', always ready to respond to His promptings.

When the starting point for your SOAP is something you have observed rather than a Scripture, don't be surprised if God then brings something from Scripture to mind as you write or contemplate, especially as you become more familiar with the Bible. No lesson from nature or a life situation will contradict Scripture if it's from the Holy Spirit. The Bible therefore is a safeguard as you learn to recognise the voice of your Saviour more instinctively.

As you can see, SOAP is about so much more than just reading the Bible. It's about listening to and communing with God. All of life is an opportunity to learn when the Holy Spirit is your teacher. If you pause and reflect, God will speak.

SOAP #14 PAUSE

Something I Noticed

A sign by a pedestrian crossing in the township of Kaikoura.

Observations

The sign by the pedestrian crossing says, 'PAUSE'. Offering no further explanation, it simply asks pedestrians to stop for a moment.

How refreshing, to expect people to figure it out themselves! *It's a crossing point. There may be cars coming. Have a look before you cross because if you mindlessly carry on without stopping for a moment to think, you might get run over!*

Application

'Pause' is a very helpful word. It could be a theme for the year ahead. *Don't mindlessly just 'keep on keeping on', I tell myself. Stop for a moment and think! Why am I doing this? Why am I doing it this way? Is there a better way to do it? Should I be doing it at all?*

'Pause' invites me to stop and think! To re-evaluate. To consider doing something differently.

'Pause' also reminds me to take time. Take time to consider another person's point of view. Take time to listen for the Holy Spirit's promptings. Take time to let the dust settle. Take time to appreciate beauty. Take time to step aside for a moment and look at what I'm doing from a different angle.

Finally, 'pause' reminds me that it's okay to rest. To pause is wise, and it is good.

Prayer

Thank You, Holy Spirit, for drawing this word to my attention. At this, the beginning of a new year, help me to pause. I pray for wisdom as I consider all my ways and as I endeavour to make 'pause' my catchcry for the year ahead.

FIFTEEN — HOT BREAD AND HONEY DEW

When I was growing up, my parents bought our bread from the supermarket. You could also buy it from the corner 'dairy' or store. Neither of those places actually baked the bread themselves. Rather, it was made in large commercial bakeries early each morning and delivered to the shops in trucks and vans. So, if you wanted to buy bread, it was the supermarket or the dairy.

Hot Bread

It was a few years later when something radical appeared in our suburb—a Hot Bread Shop! In the Hot Bread Shop, they made the bread out the back and sold it straight from the oven. Their bread was not only fresh—it was still warm. What a treat that was! I still remember the crisp, flaky crust and the way the butter melted as you spread it onto the soft, warm bread. Hot bread was the best! Having enjoyed bread straight from the oven, supermarket bread no longer seemed quite as good. It was okay, but hot bread was definitely better.

When God brought the children of Israel out of Egypt, He led them into the desert. Out there, there was no supermarket, and there certainly wasn't a hot bread shop. The Israelites started to grumble. *What would they eat?* Little did they know that something astonishing was about to happen . . .

Toward evening, quail blew in from the desert—fresh meat, delivered to the camp. How about that! Then, the following morning, the desert floor was covered in dew. When the dew was gone, thin flakes like frost appeared. "What is it?" the people exclaimed (Exodus 16:15). The Hebrew word for "What is it?" is 'manna', so that's what they called it.

For the next forty years God provided fresh manna every morning, except for on the sabbath. White like coriander seed, manna tasted like wafers made with honey (Exodus 16:31), and would last for just one day, except for the day before the sabbath, when it would last two. Then it went off. That meant that each morning, apart from the sabbath, there was no food left from the previous day. Every day the people had to once again trust God to provide them with fresh food. And God was trustworthy. Every single morning, there was 'fresh bread'. God was His people's Hot Bread Shop.

He still is.

God's 'hot bread shop' is open to you every day without fail. Fresh bread from heaven is your privilege and will not only sustain and strengthen you; it will bring you much joy.

When is the last time you received something fresh from God? Would you like to receive fresh 'manna' from Him today?

Fresh revelation, fresh insight, fresh guidance, a fresh touch of God's love, a fresh filling with the Holy Spirit—all these and more are available to you, not just when you attend church or meet with your small group. They are available to you every day, directly from God.

One of the great benefits of SOAP is that it causes us to pause, listen, and ponder. It is actively seeking fresh bread direct from the Baker's oven.

Notice I use the words 'actively seeking'. Yes, it is certainly true that, because God is good, He will at times surprise and delight us by delivering fresh bread straight to our door. But the consistent theme running through Scripture is that God rewards those who earnestly seek Him (Hebrews 11:6). Colossians 2:3 goes further when it tells us that all the treasures of wisdom and knowledge are hidden in Christ. Not 'found' in Christ, but 'hidden'. The treasures are there, but we must want them enough to search for them.

To 'seek' is 'to search for, to go after, to hunt for, to pursue'. It takes some action on our part, just as it did for the Israelites. When God delivered manna in the desert, the people still had to go out and collect it. Otherwise, they would remain hungry.

Many passages in Scripture highlight the rewards available for those whose hearts are set on pursuing Him. For example, Proverbs 2:1-6 says:

*My son, if you accept my words and store up my commands within you, turning your ear to wisdom and applying your heart to understanding, and if you call out for insight and cry aloud for understanding, and **if you look for it as for silver and search for it as for hidden treasure,** then you will understand the fear of the Lord and find the knowledge of God. For the Lord gives wisdom, and from his mouth come knowledge and understanding. (emphasis mine)*

And Isaiah 55:1-3 says:

*Come, all you who are thirsty, come to the waters; and you who have no money, **come, buy and eat!** Come, buy wine and milk without money and without cost. Why spend money on what is not bread, and your labour on what does not satisfy? Listen, listen to me, and eat what is good, and your soul will* *delight in the richest of fare.* **Give ear and come to me;** *hear me, that your soul may live. (emphasis mine)*

What wonderful invitations these are! There is no need to ever go hungry when you are in Christ. Fresh living bread is available to you every day. *Do you want to delight in the richest of fare?* Don't settle for the supermarket or the dairy any longer. God's 'hot bread shop' is open for you—now, and every day for the rest of your life.

Honey Dew

In the South Island of New Zealand where I live, many native forest areas contain beech trees. A black, sooty mould coats the trunks, and from that mould, small white tubules protrude like fine hairs. At the end of these tubules, drops of a sweet, sticky liquid form: honey dew. And just like its name suggests, it does taste like honey!

But what is honey dew?

Honey dew is a sugary substance made in the leaves of the tree. It flows down the tree through the phloem, just under the bark, providing food for the whole tree. But it sustains more than just the tree. Tiny scale insects crawl into crevices in the bark, plunge their mouthparts into the phloem, and begin to feed on the sugary liquid. Once they have connected to this constantly flowing source of food, they no longer need either legs or wings, so they shed them.

However, there is so much of the sugary food flowing into their bodies that they can't contain it. Since they have more than enough for themselves, (and in order to stop themselves from swelling up and exploding), they have to let the excess pass right on through. Happily, a white waxy tubule at their back end provides a convenient outflow for the honey dew. These tubules are what we see protruding from the sooty coating of the tree. The sooty mould itself feeds on this excess honey dew, along with numerous birds and insects. Because honey dew flows all year round, it provides a welcome food for birds over the winter months.

So, it seems that everyone is blessed by the tree, but it's the scale insect that makes that blessing accessible for all the other forest inhabitants.

We can learn a lot from the scale insect—find the source of all blessing, plug in, and never leave. This sounds a lot like what Jesus said in John 15:5 when He told us: "I am the vine; you are the branches. If a man remains in me and I in him, he will bear much fruit; apart from me you can do nothing."

Jesus is asking us to be like the scale insect. The scale insect seeks food for itself yet can't help but be a blessing to others. There is so much goodness in the tree it can't be contained. The same is true of our relationship with God. If you dig into God and feed on all the good things He has for you, you can't help but bless others too. It just overflows!

It's natural for a follower of Jesus to want to bless others. It's in our DNA! So why do some people get burnt out doing this? And why do others seem to lose their effectiveness? Because feeding others has become their first priority.

Learn from the scale insect: *Feed yourself first*. Then, you can bless others with the overflow. This is not being selfish. Rather, it is a fact of the Kingdom. If you remain in Jesus, you will bear much fruit. Apart from Him you can do nothing.

The pre-flight safety briefing on a plane will often include the following directive: "Should an oxygen mask drop down from above, please place this over your mouth and nose and breathe normally. If you have children with you, place your own mask on first before attending to the children."

It's very important, that last bit. If you try attending to your children first, you will soon find that, due to lack of oxygen, you are of no use to them at all.

The same is true of the life-giving 'oxygen' from heaven. To have any hope of sharing the blessing of God with others, you must first ensure that your own oxygen mask is fitted securely in place. Otherwise, you will soon find yourself of no use to anyone at all.

George Müller discovered these secrets for himself in the 19th century. After a wild start to life, he surrendered his life to Jesus and became a small-time minister with big aspirations. He wanted people to know that the God of the Bible is the same today as He always was, and that we can trust Him to provide for all our needs. We simply need to ask Him. Over the course of his life, he personified this message, asking God daily for what he needed, and becoming a prolific blesser of others. Though he needed every day to teach and encourage others, he made feeding himself his first priority. What he found was that if he sought God for himself, there was always enough overflow to share with and nourish others.

In feeding himself first, George Müller also fed his faith in the ability of God to provide. He built orphanages large enough to house over two thousand children, not to mention feeding them and providing for all their needs. 121,000 pupils studied at schools that he funded through a society he set up, 281,000 Bibles and 1.4 million New Testaments were printed and distributed, several hundred missionaries were financially supported to varying degrees, and he funded the printing and distribution of 111 million scriptural books, pamphlets, and tracts.

Müller was able to do all this despite having no formal income. He never had a salary, and never asked anyone for money. He never publicised his needs and never took up an offering, but simply prayed in faith and asked God directly for everything he needed.

And God answered him. The orphanages themselves were a testimony in his generation that God is alive and that He does indeed supply our needs when we pray in faith. As a result, many were inspired to a more vital and living faith in God.

Do you want to inspire and bless others? Would you like to be a channel for God's goodness? The message is clear: if you want to bless others, you must *first feed yourself*. This is exactly what you achieve when you use SOAP. By nourishing yourself in the pages of God's written Word, you will not only be blessed yourself, but the blessing of God will overflow from you to others, to the glory of God.

~

It's been over a decade since I began regularly using SOAP for my times with God in the Bible. I certainly don't want to give the impression that I have lived that time in a state of perpetual bliss, but the intimacy that I am finding with God is real and growing, and through SOAP, I am regularly gaining access to the 'hot bread and honey dew' I crave. I've discovered His Word is not just sustaining 'manna'; it is also sweetness for the soul—and that sweetness cannot be kept to ourselves. It needs to be shared. My prayer is that through this simple practice, God's Word will come alive to you and that you, like me, will be drawn closer to His heart and will delight in the richest of fare.

Taste and see that the LORD is good; blessed is the one who takes refuge in Him.
Psalm 34:8

SOAP #15: FRUIT OF A LIFE WELL SPENT

The following SOAP is one I wrote shortly after the death of my father. As I reflected on both the Scripture and my dad's memory, God allowed me to taste the sweetness of His love. The SOAP that resulted is one I will always treasure.

Reading: Galatians 5:16-26

Scripture

But the fruit of the Spirit is love, joy, peace, forbearance, kindness, goodness, faithfulness, gentleness and self-control. Against such things there is no law.

Galatians 5:22-23

Observations

Fruit doesn't appear instantly like gifts do. It grows. Most fruit starts out as a bud which soon opens into a pretty flower. The flower is only temporary though, and once pollinated, its petals fall, and its base begins to swell and grow until eventually it becomes a fully grown fruit. Even then the fruit has to ripen before it is perfect and ready to consume.

The work of the Spirit in my life is the same. The fruit is really His fruit, but I get to bear it and thereby share in the blessing of that fruit. This requires my full cooperation, and a willingness to submit to the Holy Spirit and join with Him in His work. Much fruit may be born along the way as I walk with Him, but the choicest fruit will be that which has had a lifetime to mature and ripen, perfected perhaps by suffering, and ultimately bringing glory to God through Jesus whose perfect sacrifice made it all possible.

Application

My father died this week at the age of eighty-five. As a boy he committed his life to Jesus, and he loved and served God unswervingly all of his life. Every year when I was growing up, he used to buy boxes and boxes of fresh fruit in season—apricots, plums, peaches, pears, nectarines and more. When the fruit was ripe to perfection, he would preserve it in big jars and fill our cupboards with fruit for the year ahead.

On reflection, it seems to me that his life too was characterised by fruit, of two types. The first was fruit born by him as he faithfully used his gifts and his time to serve and bless others in all sorts of ways. The second was fruit born in him, those 'character' fruit described in Galatians 5:22 which over the course of his life developed and matured, and were finally ripened to near perfection.

Perhaps the two types of fruit are one and the same, with the former being simply the natural expression of the latter. Both are evidence of a life well spent—a life committed to Jesus and yielded to the Spirit—and the fruit of his life will be enjoyed forever.

Prayer

Thank You, Lord Jesus, for the kindness and love that You have shown to my family. I thank You for the life of my father, and for the legacy that he has passed down to his children. May good fruit continue to fill our cupboards and overflow in expressions of thankfulness and praise to You.

EPILOGUE: STARTING A NEW HABIT

When I was young, I lived over the fence from a horse paddock. The gravel drive leading to the paddock passed through a small overgrown wasteland of long, thick grass. One day my friends and I struck on the brilliant idea of making a narrow windy track through this wasteland on which to race around on our bikes. The problem was, it was impossible to ride through the grass. It was so long and thick, our bikes would simply stop and we'd fall off. In fact, it was all we could do just to push our bikes through the grass.

But we were determined, so we did just that. We pushed our bikes through the long grass, over and over. Each time around, the grass on our fledgling track became a little bit flatter as we repeatedly trampled it down and pushed our bikes over it, but we still couldn't ride through it. We decided to come back the next day and do it again. Over the course of a fortnight, the trampled grass route began to look more and more like a track. We could ride around it now, albeit slowly. Sometimes we fell off, but with each lap, our tyres squashed the flattened grass deeper into the dirt. It became easier and easier to ride around. Instead of long thick grass, or even a grassy mat, we had hard-packed dirt. And so it was that after a month of repeated riding, our track was complete. We were racing.

Sometimes, starting a new habit can feel a bit like trying to ride your bike through long grass. It seems impossible, and it's tempting to give up when you've hardly even started. But if you're persistent, you'll start to wear a track, and gradually it will become easier and easier.

Meeting with God in the Bible is like that. Sometimes, it can be hard at first, and you might feel like giving up. But if you keep at it for long enough, it will get easier and easier. Having someone to team up with can help—like I did all those years ago, you could enlist the help of a buddy, or even a group to help you carve out a path.

But whether with someone else or solo, determine that you will 'ride your bike through the grass' as often as you can. God will be cheering you on, and soon enough, you will be racing.

AUTHOR'S NOTE

I hope you have enjoyed this book. I hope it has stirred and inspired you and left you hungry to know God more. My prayer for you is that God will fully satisfy your hunger for Him, and at the same time whet your appetite for more. There is always more.

It may be that, though hungry, you are yet to open your heart to God. If that is the case, thank you so much for reading this far. In some ways, your journey with God has already begun. I have shared openly in this book and have presented a clear picture of what a relationship with God can look like when you pursue Him with all your heart.

Now it is up to you.

To begin a new life with God at the centre, simply come as you are and surrender your life to Him. Confess to Him your need for forgiveness, and He will make you clean. Offer to Him your brokenness, and He will restore you. Submit to Jesus as Lord of your life, and let Him lead you and guide you from this day forward.

Don't try to earn God's love. You can't. Instead, accept for yourself the most costly free gift ever given, knowing that Jesus has done everything required to enable you to stand in God's presence, holy, accepted, and loved.

There's a simple prayer I often pray: "Lord, soften their hearts to hear Your voice and respond."

No matter where you are on your journey with God, this prayer encapsulates what a relationship with Him is all about—having your heart inclined towards Him to hear His voice and willingly respond with obedience and gratitude. This is my own life's pursuit, and as you come to the end of this book, I pray that it might become yours also. And so, I leave you with this blessing:

May God soften your heart to hear His voice and respond. May the love of Jesus fill you, may the Holy Spirit be your ever-present companion, and may God's intimate friendship bless your house forever.

—Simon Dodge

RECOMMENDED RESOURCES

The Essential 100 Challenge

- *www.bible.com/en/reading-plans/25-the-essential-100*
- *www.youversion.com/reading-plans/the-essential-100-challenge*
- *www.bible.com/reading-plans/2453-essential-scripture-for-30-days*

The Bible Project

- *www.bibleproject.com/explore/book-overviews*

Bible Reading Plan

- *www.biblestudytools.com/bible-reading-plan*

APPENDIX 1: UNDERSTANDING THE STRUCTURE OF THE BIBLE

This book, *Sneaking Off With God*, was written to help you find intimacy with God though the Bible. Rather than being a resource book on the content, structure and history of the Bible, it is intended to sit beside and complement such resources. The following paragraphs therefore contain just a few brief facts, anticipating that you will seek and find further information elsewhere.

The Bible is a remarkable book. It is, in fact, made up of sixty-six books written by forty authors over a period of about sixteen hundred years. It contains history and poetry, prophesy and statistics, letters and stories—some heart-warming and others gruesome. There are heroes and villains and ordinary people like us making up a rich contingent of characters who between them provide both shining examples for us to emulate and lessons of what not to do. What is remarkable is that God can speak through it all!

The first five books of the Bible, referred to as the 'Torah' or the 'Pentateuch', consist largely of history, covering the beginnings of life and the universe, the flood, and the origins of the nation of Israel, which forms a central part in the narrative of God's dealings with mankind.

Following on from these books, we discover further historical accounts, poetry, songs, and the wisdom books as well as the writings of many prophets. Rather than following strict chronological order, the books are grouped together by genre, which means when you are reading the prophets, they may refer to historical events found in earlier books such as Samuel, Kings and Chronicles, or they may point forward to future events. Some prophetic writings may even have dual meanings, speaking to both the present and the future.

After the last book in the Old Testament, Malachi, there is a gap of over four hundred years. All sorts of interesting geopolitical events were occurring during this in-between time, including the rise and fall of empires and the establishment of common languages. Roads were built, literally paving the way for the arrival of Jesus and the spread of the gospel far and wide. Ending this period of silence in the Scriptures, the New Testament begins with the

Gospels—four different but complementary accounts of the life of Jesus—before moving on to an historical account of the spread of the early church following Jesus' resurrection in the book of Acts. Next follows a collection of letters written to various churches and individuals to help them understand how to live out their faith. The final book in the Bible is Revelation, being the revelation of Jesus Christ given to John during his imprisonment on the island of Patmos. John was the only one of Jesus' twelve disciples (aside from Judas Iscariot) who was not martyred for his faith—despite Rome's best efforts. He recorded the revelation in about 90AD.

When thinking about the Bible and how it is put together, it's useful to remember that the church suffered much persecution during the first three centuries of its existence, and as a result, it wasn't easy for church leaders scattered across countries and continents to get together to talk. It took a few centuries, along with much prayer and wisdom, for the early church to finally determine what should be included in the so-called 'canon' of Scripture. Christians believe that just as God inspired the writers of the Bible, He also determined what would be included in it. Though we human beings are fallible, God is sovereign, and well able to achieve His perfect will through us.

It's worth reflecting on the fact that for long periods of time, the Bible was not available for the average person to read. Only a privileged few had possession of it, and often in a language such as Latin that most people couldn't read. This time in history was known as the Dark Ages. When John Wycliffe and others began translating the Bible into English in the late 1300s, church leaders of the day feared what might happen if the average person could read the Bible for themselves in their own language—so much so that they tried to kill Wycliffe and he had to flee to France.

Eventually an English Bible was translated, and a copy put in every English-speaking church. People were so hungry to read these Bibles that they had to be chained down or people would steal them. Not until the publishing of the King James Version in 1611 did the Scriptures become widely available to readers of English. A little over four hundred years later, the Bible has been translated into about four thousand languages, and in English, countless translations are now available. Yet even with all that progress, three thousand people groups still wait to read the Bible in their own tongue.

APPENDIX 2: HOW TO READ THE BIBLE

If the Bible was a novel, there would be no need to ask where to start—you would simply start at the beginning and finish at the end. If it was a magazine, you might go straight to the article that most interested you, or just flick through the pages, waiting for something to catch your eye. If it was a textbook, you would search for your topic of interest in the table of contents or the index at the back. And if it was just a collection of writings spread across the internet, you might do a google search and hope for the best.

The Bible is none of those things, yet all of these approaches have been used to read it. So how and where should you start? The purpose of this appendix is to answer that question, helping you to start well (or perhaps restart well), and then get into a Bible-reading groove you can continue for life. Whether you're new to the Bible or are restarting after a long hiatus, my suggestion is that you begin by reading a few of the Bible's key books, then do a reading overview before settling into a Bible-reading rhythm that will work for you long term. Allow me to elaborate.

Read a Few Key Books

If you're new to the Bible, reading a few of its key books is a great way to start. I'd suggest that you begin with one of the Gospels and get familiar with Jesus and His teachings—Mark and John are both great books to start with. Another key book is Genesis. All about beginnings and origins, it records the history of how the world began, establishes God's purpose for mankind, and provides context for everything else in the Bible.

The Book of Acts is another important early-read. Acts gives an historical account of the activities of the early church and the spread of the gospel as the first Christians explored what it meant to be the church, and to live out the 'great commission' that Jesus had given them. The same is true of Paul's letter to the Ephesians. This short book reveals much of God's love and purpose for the church and provides practical instruction on living out our faith. If you're not sure how to find these books in the 'library' that is the Bible, you can look them up in the contents page at the front of your Bible. Don't feel obliged to use the SOAP format immediately. Just read and start to orient yourself to the story of Scripture.

Getting the Lay of the Land

Once you've read some of these 'cornerstone' books, it can be helpful to get an overview of Scripture as a whole—particularly if you're not familiar with the Bible or have read little of it for yourself.

Now before you start to feel overwhelmed, I am not suggesting that you read from Genesis to Revelation straight out of the gate. That is a daunting task which I would liken to doing a jigsaw puzzle in the dark without having seen the picture on the front of the box—not impossible, but certainly difficult! A much better way to get an overview of the Bible is to start with a 'fly over' approach. There are a few ways to do this. One is to read (or watch or listen to) a 'Beginner's Guide to the Bible'. The other is to read a selection of key passages from the Bible itself using a Bible-reading plan.

At the end of this book, you will find one I recommend. It's called the Essential 100 Challenge (or, E100 Bible Reading Plan). Put out by Scripture Union, the E100 plan is a sort of 'highlights package', giving readers a list of one hundred 'essential' passages—fifty key readings from the Old Testament and fifty from the New Testament.

I encourage you to use both approaches together. That way, you'll have a good sense of the 'lie of land' when it comes to the Bible, and you'll also get to experience the highlights. Later, when you're ready to parachute in for a closer look, you'll know exactly where you are. Even more importantly, you will begin to establish a consistent Bible-reading habit that will stand you in good stead for the years ahead.

Finding a Rhythm that Works

Once you've got a good overview of the Bible, you'll want to get into a regular reading rhythm that enables you to enjoy the whole Bible, whilst keeping things fresh and not locking you into an impossible reading schedule.

Keep in mind that the whole Bible is inspired by God, and the more you read it, the more treasure you'll discover within it, often in the most unexpected places. Sometimes you'll feast at the bountiful table of Ephesians—other times, you'll saddle up your camel and head out into the badlands of Ezekiel in search of rare delights.

If we think of the Bible as a complete and balanced diet, there are two possible approaches we could take to reading it. One is 'à la carte' where you choose one item from the menu and eat until you're finished. The other is more like a buffet where you take a little from each of a large selection of dishes, only to return later for another round. Let's look at each of those approaches, along with their pros and cons.

One Book at a Time

The 'à la carte' approach is to choose a single book from the Bible and work through it until you're finished before moving on to another. Ideally, you would have a plan, so you know exactly which book you are going to read next. Your plan might take you through the Bible in chronological order, or alternate from Old to New Testament books, or follow some other well-reasoned progression to ensure that, in time, you cover the whole Bible.

Reading one book in the Bible from beginning to end helps with continuity and understanding. You'll get a good feel for each book, and you won't forget what was happening when you last read. Books will often have a distinct theme which might be easier to appreciate when you're reading it right through.

The Seven Loop Cycle

Having described the approach of reading one book at a time, you might wonder why you would read the Bible any other way.

But there is another excellent way to read the Bible—more like a 'meal plan' designed to fill every week with a feast of all the Bible has to offer. For want of a better description, I will call it the "Seven Loop Cycle." Allow me to explain.

In his excellent 'Rainbow Bible Guide', author and teacher John Fergusson presents a simple Bible-reading plan that uses a seven-loop cycle :

- *Loop One: Genesis to Deuteronomy (History and Law)*
- *Loop Two: Matthew to Luke (Gospels)*
- *Loop Three: Joshua to Esther (History)*
- *Loop Four: Romans to Jude (Letters)*
- *Loop Five: Isaiah to Malachi (Prophets)*
- *Loop Six: John, Acts and Revelation (Writings)*
- *Loop Seven: Job to Song of Songs (Poetry)*

On your first day, you read from loop one, starting in Genesis. On your next reading day, you go to loop two and start reading Matthew. Next reading day, it's loop three starting with Joshua, and so on. After loop seven, you simply go back to loop one and pick up where you left off in Genesis, then to loop two and pick up where you left off in Matthew—and so it continues. You're effectively working through seven consecutive loops, some of which will take longer to read through than others—but that doesn't matter. When you eventually reach the end of any one loop, you simply go back and start that loop again.

The advantage of using the Seven Loop Cycle or a reading plan like it, is that it helps you consistently read from both the Old and New Testaments and takes you systematically through the whole Bible. Plus, if you find yourself in a 'dry' patch, you won't get stuck there since you'll be reading a different book the next day—and the next! Even if you take a break from the rhythm to read one book right through or to explore a topic (you'll likely do both), once you're finished you can simply pick up right where you left off. In this way, the Seven Loop Cycle remains in place as your default setting, meaning you'll never be scratching your head thinking, *What shall I read next?*

Seven loops obviously lends itself nicely to a one week reading cycle. If you are blessed with the opportunity to read long sections of the Bible every day, seize that opportunity with both hands! If not, just work through the seven loops in order at your own pace, reading as much or as little as you are able. And of course, once you're familiar with it, you can use SOAP to help you unwrap something each time you read. I use this plan myself and am amazed at how God will speak to me on a particular theme across different parts of the Bible, and on different days.

Both approaches to Bible reading have potential downsides, especially for less frequent readers. When reading just one book at a time, it's easy to avoid reading the 'harder' books and thereby miss some of what God wants to show you in the Bible. And while a loop cycle avoids this pitfall, you lose a little of the continuity of Scripture and may need to remind yourself what was happening when you last read that specific loop before getting back into it. My personal advice is this: choose the best of both worlds! Have a plan that regularly takes you through the whole Bible but allow yourself the freedom to zero in on a particular book or topic as the Holy Spirit piques your interest. This will mean that you'll know some parts of Scripture very well, others less so, but none will be unvisited.

Remember that more important than the plan itself, is simply being consistent. Any balanced reading plan that enables you to regularly and reliably draw close to God, hear His voice, and find intimacy with Him, is achieving its purpose.

Setting the Right Goals

People often ask me how much of the Bible they should aim to read each day. Again, there is no single answer. The quantity doesn't matter, because your goal is not to read a certain number of chapters per day—it is to meet with God and learn from Him. After God brought the Israelites out of Egypt, they spent forty years in the desert. During that time, they did not follow a timetable; they followed a pillar. By day, it was a pillar of cloud, giving them shade, and by night it was a pillar of fire, giving light and warmth. God was in the pillar. When it stopped, the Israelites stopped. When it moved on, the Israelites moved on.

You can do the same as you read the Bible. If the 'pillar of fire' stops three times in the same chapter, awesome! Set up camp. Let this be your Tent of Meeting until you've enjoyed all that God has for you in those Scriptures. But if the Holy Spirit brings nothing to your attention, that's fine. Let God determine how quickly or slowly you move along.

Some people like to set themselves a goal of reading a certain number of chapters per day, or of reading the Bible in a year. If this works for you, go for it. Having a target can provide motivation to keep at it, so long as the target is achievable. But if your reading target is taking over from the pillar of fire, that's a problem. Why not let the Tour Guide decide how long you will stop in each place? Then you will have plenty of time to ponder and ruminate and worship, and you will achieve your goal of finding intimacy with God.

I want to offer a word of encouragement for the 'time-poor'. For many people, a dedicated time with God each day to read the Bible and do a SOAP is a luxury. If only! It's easy to feel guilty if you have set yourself an expectation you can't meet. Please, don't. The Holy Spirit encourages, He does not condemn. Each of life's seasons brings its own challenges and its own blessings. So shake off any condemnation you feel, and enjoy the opportunities you do have, remembering His plan for your life is that you:

"Be joyful always; pray continually; give thanks in all circumstances, for this is God's will for you in Christ Jesus."
1 Thessalonians 5:16-18

APPENDIX 3: THE ESSENTIAL ONE HUNDRED CHALLENGE

Old Testament

IN THE BEGINNING
- ☐ 1. Creation — Genesis 1.1-2.25
- ☐ 2. The Fall — Genesis 3.1-24
- ☐ 3. The Flood — Genesis 6.5-7.24
- ☐ 4. God's Covenant with Noah — Genesis 8.1-9.17
- ☐ 5. Tower of Babel — Genesis 11.1-9

ABRAHAM, ISAAC AND JACOB
- ☐ 6. The Call of Abram — Genesis 12.1-20
- ☐ 7. God's Covenant with Abram — Genesis 15.1-21
- ☐ 8. Isaac's Birth and "Sacrifice" — Genesis 21.1-22.19
- ☐ 9. Jacob and Esau Compete — Genesis 27.1-28.22
- ☐ 10. Jacob and Esau Reconcile — Genesis 32.1-33.20

THE STORY OF JOSEPH
- ☐ 11. Sold Into Slavery — Genesis 37.1-36
- ☐ 12. Prison and a Promotion — Genesis 39.1-41.57
- ☐ 13. Ten Brothers Go to Egypt — Genesis 42.1-38
- ☐ 14. The Brothers Return — Genesis 43.1-44.34
- ☐ 15. Joseph Reveals His Identity — Genesis 45.1-46.7

MOSES AND THE EXODUS
- ☐ 16. Birth of Moses — Exodus 1.1-2.25
- ☐ 17. The Burning Bush — Exodus 3.1-4.17
- ☐ 18. The Ten Plagues — Exodus 6.28-11.10
- ☐ 19. Passover and Exodus — Exodus 12.1-42
- ☐ 20. Crossing the Red Sea — Exodus 13.17-14.31

THE LAW AND THE LAND
- ☐ 21. The Ten Commandments — Exodus 19.1-20.21
- ☐ 22. The Golden Calf — Exodus 32.1-34.35
- ☐ 23. Joshua Succeeds Moses — Joshua 1.1-18
- ☐ 24. Crossing the Jordan — Joshua 3.1-4.24
- ☐ 25. Fall of Jericho — Joshua 5.13-6.27

THE JUDGES
- ☐ 26. Israel's Disobedience — Judges 2.6-3.6
- ☐ 27. Deborah Leads Israel — Judges 4.1-5.31
- ☐ 28. Gideon Defeats the Midianites — Judges 6.1-7.25
- ☐ 29. Samson Defeats the Philistines — Judges 13.1-16.31
- ☐ 30. The Story of Ruth — Ruth 1.1-4.22

THE RISE OF ISRAEL
- ☐ 31. Samuel Listens to God — 1 Samuel 1.1-3.21
- ☐ 32. King Saul — 1 Samuel 8.1-10.27
- ☐ 33. David and Goliath — 1 Samuel 16.1-18.16
- ☐ 34. David and Saul — 1 Samuel 23.7-24.22
- ☐ 35. King David — 2 Samuel 5.1-7.29

THE FALL OF ISRAEL
- ☐ 36. David and Bathsheba — 2 Samuel 11.1-12.25
- ☐ 37. King Solomon — 1 Kings 2.1-3.28
- ☐ 38. Solomon's Temple — 1 Kings 8.1-9.9
- ☐ 39. Elijah and the Prophets of Baal — 1 Kings 16.29-19.18
- ☐ 40. The Fall of Jerusalem — 2 Kings 25.1-30

PSALMS AND PROVERBS
- ☐ 41. The Lord is My Shepherd — Psalm 23.1-6
- ☐ 42. Have Mercy on Me — Psalm 51.1-19
- ☐ 43. Praise the Lord — Psalm 103.1-22
- ☐ 44. Godly Wisdom — Proverbs 1.1-4.27
- ☐ 45. Proverbs of Solomon — Proverbs 16.1-18.24

THE PROPHETS
- ☐ 46. The Suffering Servant — Isaiah 51.1-53.12
- ☐ 47. Jeremiah's Call and Message — Jeremiah 1.1-3.5
- ☐ 48. Daniel in the Lion's Den — Daniel 6.1-28
- ☐ 49. The Story of Jonah — Jonah 1.1-4.11
- ☐ 50. The Day of Judgment — Malachi 1.1-4.6

New Testament

THE LIVING WORD
- ☐ 51. The Word Became Flesh — John 1.1-18
- ☐ 52. Gabriel's Message — Luke 1.1-80
- ☐ 53. The Birth of Jesus — Luke 2.1-40
- ☐ 54. John the Baptist — Luke 3.1-20
- ☐ 55. Baptism and Temptation — Matthew 3.13-4.17

THE TEACHINGS OF JESUS
- ☐ 56. Sermon on the Mount - Part 1 — Matthew 5.1-6.4
- ☐ 57. Sermon on the Mount - Part 2 — Matthew 6.5-7.29
- ☐ 58. The Kingdom of Heaven — Matthew 13.1-58
- ☐ 59. The Good Samaritan — Luke 10.25-37
- ☐ 60. Lost and Found — Luke 15.1-32

THE MIRACLES OF JESUS
- ☐ 61. Feeding the Five Thousand — Luke 9.1-36
- ☐ 62. Walking on Water — Matthew 14.22-36
- ☐ 63. Healing a Blind Man — John 9.1-41
- ☐ 64. Healing a Demon-Possessed Man — Mark 5.1-20
- ☐ 65. Raising Lazarus from the Dead — John 11.1-57

THE CROSS OF CHRIST
- ☐ 66. The Last Supper — Luke 22.1-46
- ☐ 67. Arrest and Trial — John 18.1-40
- ☐ 68. The Crucifixion — John 19.1-42
- ☐ 69. The Resurrection — John 20.1-21.25
- ☐ 70. The Ascension — Acts 1.1-11

THE CHURCH IS BORN
- ☐ 71. The Day of Pentecost — Acts 2.1-47
- ☐ 72. Growth and Persecution — Acts 3.1-4.37
- ☐ 73. The First Martyr — Acts 6.8-8.8
- ☐ 74. Sharing the Word — Acts 8.26-40
- ☐ 75. Good News for All — Acts 10.1-11.18

THE TRAVELS OF PAUL
- ☐ 76. The Road to Damascus — Acts 9.1-31
- ☐ 77. The First Missionary Journey — Acts 13.1-14.28
- ☐ 78. The Council at Jerusalem — Acts 15.1-41
- ☐ 79. More Missionary Journeys — Acts 16.1-20.38
- ☐ 80. The Trip to Rome — Acts 25.1-28.31

PAUL TO THE CHURCHES
- ☐ 81. More than Conquerors — Romans 8.1-39
- ☐ 82. The Fruit of the Spirit — Galatians 5.16-6.10
- ☐ 83. The Armor of God — Ephesians 6.10-20
- ☐ 84. Rejoice in the Lord — Philippians 4.2-9
- ☐ 85. The Supremacy of Christ — Colossians 1.1-23

PAUL TO THE LEADERS
- ☐ 86. Elders and Deacons — 1 Timothy 3.1-16
- ☐ 87. The Love of Money — 1 Timothy 6.3-21
- ☐ 88. Good Soldiers of Christ — 2 Timothy 2.1-26
- ☐ 89. All Scripture is God-Breathed — 2 Timothy 3.10-4.8
- ☐ 90. The Coming of the Lord — 1 Thessalonians 4.13-5.11

THE APOSTLES' TEACHING
- ☐ 91. The Most Excellent Way — 1 Corinthians 13.1-13
- ☐ 92. A New Creation in Christ — 2 Corinthians 4.1-6.2
- ☐ 93. A Living Hope — 1 Peter 1.1-2.12
- ☐ 94. Faith and Works — James 1.1-2.26
- ☐ 95. Love One Another — 1 John 3.11-4.21

THE REVELATION
- ☐ 96. A Voice and a Vision — Revelation 1.1-20
- ☐ 97. Messages to the Churches — Revelation 2.1-3.22
- ☐ 98. The Throne of Heaven — Revelation 4.1-7.17
- ☐ 99. Hallelujah! — Revelation 19.1-20.15
- ☐ 100. The New Jerusalem — Revelation 21.1-22.21